Tucholsky Wagner Zola Scott Sydow Freud Schlegel
Turgenev Wallace Fonatne Friedrich II. von Preußen
Twain Walther von der Vogelweide Fouqué
Weber Freiligrath Frey
Kant Ernst
Fechner Fichte Weiße Rose von Fallersleben Richthofen Frommel
Hölderlin
Engels Fielding Eichendorff Tacitus Dumas
Fehrs Faber Flaubert
Eliasberg Ebner Eschenbach
Maximilian I. von Habsburg Fock Zweig
Feuerbach Eliot Vergil
Ewald
Goethe London
Elisabeth von Österreich
Mendelssohn Balzac Shakespeare Dostojewski Ganghofer
Lichtenberg Rathenau Doyle Gjellerup
Trackl Stevenson Hambruch
Mommsen Tolstoi Lenz Droste-Hülshoff
Thoma Hanrieder
von Arnim Hägele Hauff Humboldt
Dach Verne Hagen Hauptmann Gautier
Reuter Rousseau
Karrillon Garschin Baudelaire
Defoe
Damaschke Descartes Hebbel
Hegel Kussmaul Herder
Wolfram von Eschenbach Dickens Schopenhauer
Darwin Melville Grimm Jerome Rilke George
Bronner Bebel Proust
Campe Horváth Aristoteles Federer
Voltaire Herodot
Bismarck Vigny Barlach Heine
Gengenbach
Storm Casanova Tersteegen Grillparzer Georgy
Gilm
Chamberlain Lessing Langbein Gryphius
Brentano Lafontaine
Strachwitz Claudius Schiller Kralik Iffland Sokrates
Schilling
Katharina II. von Rußland Bellamy
Gerstäcker Raabe Gibbon Tschechow
Löns Hesse Hoffmann Gogol Wilde Vulpius
Gleim
Luther Heym Hofmannsthal Morgenstern
Klee Hölty Goedicke
Roth Heyse Klopstock Kleist
Luxemburg Puschkin Homer Mörike
La Roche Horaz Musil
Machiavelli Kierkegaard Kraft Kraus
Navarra Aurel Musset
Lamprecht Kind Moltke
Nestroy Marie de France Kirchhoff Hugo
Laotse Ipsen Liebknecht
Nietzsche Nansen Ringelnatz
Marx
von Ossietzky Lassalle Gorki Klett Leibniz
May vom Stein Lawrence Irving
Petalozzi Knigge
Platon
Sachs Pückler Michelangelo Kafka
Poe Kock
Liebermann Korolenko
de Sade Praetorius Mistral Zetkin

The publishing house tredition has created the series **TREDITION CLASSICS**. It contains classical literature works from over two thousand years. Most of these titles have been out of print and off the bookstore shelves for decades.

The book series is intended to preserve the cultural legacy and to promote the timeless works of classical literature. As a reader of a **TREDITION CLASSICS** book, the reader supports the mission to save many of the amazing works of world literature from oblivion.

The symbol of **TREDITION CLASSICS** is Johannes Gutenberg (1400 – 1468), the inventor of movable type printing.

With the series, tredition intends to make thousands of international literature classics available in printed format again – worldwide.

All books are available at book retailers worldwide in paperback and in hardcover. For more information please visit: www.tredition.com

tredition was established in 2006 by Sandra Latusseck and Soenke Schulz. Based in Hamburg, Germany, tredition offers publishing solutions to authors and publishing houses, combined with worldwide distribution of printed and digital book content. tredition is uniquely positioned to enable authors and publishing houses to create books on their own terms and without conventional manufacturing risks.

For more information please visit: www.tredition.com

Free and Impartial Thoughts, on the Sovereignty of God, The Doctrines of Election, Reprobation, and Original Sin: Humbly Addressed To all who Believe and Profess those Doctrines.

Richard Finch

Imprint

This book is part of the TREDITION CLASSICS series.

Author: Richard Finch
Cover design: toepferschumann, Berlin (Germany)

Publisher: tredition GmbH, Hamburg (Germany)
ISBN: 978-3-8491-4739-6

www.tredition.com
www.tredition.de

THE PREFACE

I Cannot find, upon the most impartial Retrospection of the Argument, any Reason to alter my Sentiments concerning it; and as it is a Matter of the greatest Importance, 'tis hoped that those who maintain the Doctrines of Election, *&c. will afford it all the Weight and Consideration it deserves. But, if there be any among them, who will hear no Reason or Argument whatever, and are* sure, only because they are sure, *I* Have little *or* no Hopes *to prevail with them, to give me a fair Hearing, or to think* candidly *and* impartially *about it. But as there are among them, some, who no doubt will allow the* Possibility *of their being in an Error; to all such I address my self, and beseech them, as much as possible to lay aside Prejudice and Partiality; wisely considering, that many of their Fore-fathers maintained some erroneous Doctrines, with as much Zeal, and Integrity, as they their Descendants now do the Doctrines of* Election, *&c. and yet saw Occasion to renounce them afterwards.*

There is Reason to fear, the just Liberty I have taken with the Doctrines of Election, *&c. may, by some, be deem'd Blasphemy against* Godhimself; *but I am far from intending any such thing. These Doctrines (I think) on the contrary, are* in them selves *nothing better than* blasphemous, tho' *the Intentions of some who maintain them, be ever so devout and sincere: And if an Impeachment of Doctrines, which, instead of preserving* God's Moral Character, *robs him of all that is dear and valuable, or that can render him lovely and adorable to Man, be accounted* Blasphemy, *the Ignorance and Bigotry of those, who judge after that Manner, ought much to be lamented. It is a melancholy Truth, that where Prejudice, in favour of false Principles, has had early and frequent Access to the Mind, it too often shuts the Ear against Reason and Truth; and 'tis very hard to persuade such People to enter at all, and much less impartially, into the Merits of an Argument advanced against them; nor indeed is the Liberty of Thought on* Religious Subjects, duly inculcated *in Religious Assemblies: For, the* Teachers of Christianity, tho' *they are seldom averse to give us the Compliment of a* just Liberty of thinking for ourselves, *are but too apt* to set the Terrors of the Lord in array against Unbelievers; tho' *perhaps* their Dissent *may sometimes be only the* innocent Effect, *of the best* Examination they are able to make. *And if there be any thing worthy of Notice, in what I have advanced, I hereby intreat all, into whose Hands this Treatise may come, not to be terrified, by any such popular Arts, from* *making a thorough Examination for themselves; on the other hand, I am altogether as willing to set right, in whatever I may have erred, or been mistaken.*

'Tis well known, the 17th Article of our own National Church, *greatly favours the* Doctrines *of* Election *and* Reprobation; *and it is also generally believed, that the* Better Part *of our Clergy entirely disapprove these Doctrines, and would very readily assist in expunging them out of their* Creed; *which would render their Consciences much easier, than now they are, or can be, under a Subscription in a Sense so* very *qualified and remote* from the natural Intent *and* Meaning *of the Article.*

Experience makes it evident, that Education is able to retain Men of the Brightest Understanding, *in the Belief of the* Greatest Absurdities. *But, that Men of Learning, Ingenuity and Experience, who have lived perhaps to the Age of fifty, in the Disbelief of the* Doctrines *of* Election, *&c. should after that sincerely embrace them, is to me Matter of great Astonishment; yet this I am inform'd is really the Case, with regard to one of the most ingenious* Divines, *our Metropolis has to boast of. One Reason may perhaps be alledged, for such an unexpected Alteration of Sentiment, viz. That tho' we disbelieve these Doctrines, because they are* absurd, *yet we hold at the same time, others,* equally repugnant *to Reason, and to Common Sense; and certainly we may as reasonably* embrace *the one as* retain *the other. Besides, with what reasonable Expectation of Success could such a Man as this sit down to argue with* another *of absurd Principles, when* he himself *might be so easily abash'd and put to Silence, by an Appeal to* other Principles, *of* his own, *equally absurd and inexplicable. The best way then, instead of embracing a* fresh, absurd, *Principle of Faith, is, to renounce the* old. *I would not willingly Offend* Any, *by a special Application to* particular Societies *and* Doctrines: *let but every Man make an honest Application to himself, and the Articles of Faith he professes, and the Work of Reformation will, I am persuaded, gain something thereby. And that, not only these Doctrines, but every other absurd Principle of Faith, which either Ignorance, or Design, may have introduced into the Christian church, to the* Dishonour *of God, the* Burthen *and* Reproach *of Human Nature, may be* utterly exploded, *is the incessant Wish, and earnest Desire, of*

The Author.

Free*and*Impartial

THOUGHTS, &c.

CHRISTIANITY having been instituted, by its great Author and Publisher, for the Benefit and Advantage of Mankind, it is pity we should so greatly differ, concerning what *Genuine Christianity* is; if the *Holy Bible*, as we generally agree, was designed to lead us to the true Knowledge of God, and to be a standing and perpetual Rule of *Faith* and *Manners* to Men, it must surely have been greatly corrupted since the primitive Times of the Gospel, or the *Explication* of it designedly left to a more excellent and superior Director: For the seeming Contradictions, and Multiplicity of obscure Passages, wherewith it abounds, shew plainly it could never, in its present Condition, be a Rule of Faith, &c. becoming an all-wise and perfect Being, to give to rational Creatures. Every *good Man, Society*, and *State*, study Perspicuity in all their *Rules, Orders, and Statutes,* dispensed to their *Families, Members,* and *Subjects:* and can we suppose, that He, who is perfect in Knowledge, would, in the Dispensation of his Laws, take less care of the everlasting State of his immortal Creature *Man?* Yet it is plain, we differ in our Sentiments of Religion, and greatly too, for want, as I sincerely hope, of the Knowledge of better Helps, to direct our Inquiries, in Matters, the true Knowledge whereof, is of so considerable Moment. Therefore,

I intend, in the Course of this Debate, to descant *freely*, on the Doctrines of *Divine Sovereignty, Election, Reprobation*, and *Original Sin;* and also, on the Arguments which some ingenious Gentlemen have used to support them. But I hope (with regard to the *Authors* I may possibly name) to be perfectly decent, and to treat them with all becoming Respect and Deference, as I think Men of Integrity, Learning and Abilities deserve; who, though in some Points they may err, and hold Doctrines in their own Nature and Tendency altogether subversive of Religion and Morality, do nevertheless not perceive them to have these Tendencies, and are therefore by *no Means* chargeable with them. Yet, as touching the *Doctrines* themselves, I shall presume to speak freely, both in regard to their Nature, and what appears to me to be their genuine Fruits and Effects.

It is with me an establish'd Truth, that the mistaken Notion of some *learned Men*, concerning the *Sovereignty* of the *Deity*, has given these Doctrines a more favourable Acceptance in the World, than otherwise they would, or could, ever have met with; and notwithstanding all the Pains and Arguments these Gentlemen have bestowed, to reconcile their Doctrines to our common Sense of *Right* and *Wrong*, it is plain, that, at *bottom*, this is the grand governing Principle. For, when their Attempts to reconcile these Doctrines with common Sense and Equity fail, they have immediate Recourse to God's *Sovereignty*, and even go so far, at least in Effect, as to deny there is *any* intrinsick Difference in Things themselves, as shall be made appear from their most approved Writers, whenever they are pleased to demand it: But as this Principle of *Sovereignty* is most certainly their strong Hold, I shall therefore endeavour to go to the Depth of this Argument; and shew, in the first Place, how greatly they misapprehend the Nature of this *Attribute;* and, in the second Place, granting it to be as they say, I shall then shew the *precarious* and *miserable* Condition of all Mankind, not excepting the Elect themselves, under the Government of such an arbitrary Being.

To begin with the first. That God is a *Sovereign*, we readily allow: But it will not therefore follow, he is *morally capable* of doing any thing, in its *own Nature*, immoral or unjust. All religious Debates are allowed to be best determinable by the divine Attributes; and yet nothing is more common, than to single out, and lay the greatest Stress on, that Attribute alone, which appears best to suit our own particular Opinions: which, however innocent our Intention may be, is, I think, in itself, a very erroneous and unwarrantable Procedure; for as God is *all-wise* and *good*, as well as *almighty* and *independent*, it is, in the Nature of Things, impossible (and therefore we should never admit it possible) he should be capable (in a moral Sense, I mean) of exerting any one particular Attribute in *Opposition* to, or *Diminution* from, another. A *Sovereign* he is, nor can any Creature whatever dispute his *unlimited* and *uncontroulable* Power over his *whole Creation*. But Power alone, without Wisdom and Goodness to make a right Use and Application of it, may be perfect *Frenzy*, and run into the greatest Latitude of *Folly* and *Tyranny*. It is, if I may be allowed the Comparison, like a *Vessel* that has lost its Helm, continually exposed to the tossing of Winds and Waves. To talk, therefore, of *mere Sovereign Pleasure*, without Regard to the proper Reason or Fitness of Things, so far operating and bring in the *Divine Mind* (and which is nothing more than the Presence and Operation of his own Wisdom) in order to prefer what, in its own Nature, is *best*, and *fittest* to be done, is excluding from the Deity, those *more* blessed and *valuable Perfections* of *Wisdom* and *Goodness*, and establishing in their room, and at their Expence, mere Sovereign Power alone. *Physically speaking* indeed, we allow God can do Evil itself; but the moral Perfections of his Nature, are to us an *infallible* and *unshaken Security*, that he *never will* do it. *Man* being an impotent and fallible Creature, liable, not only to mistake the true Nature and importance of Things, but when he does understand his Duty rightly, liable also, thro' the Prevalence of *Habit* and *Passion*, to be very backward and defective in performing it, must necessarily be subject to such Laws, as contain in them Rewards and Punishments, proper to influence his *Hopes* and his *Fears*.

But as God, on the contrary, is a Being of all possible and infinite Perfections; an exact Knowledge of what we call *Right* and *Wrong*, *Just* and *Unjust*, ever hath, and always will exit in the *Divine Mind*, and be to him a perfect, constant, and invariable Rule of Action, in relation to his Creatures. He that is *infinite* in Knowledge, cannot but know, at all Times, and under the most (to us) difficult and perplex'd Circumstances of Things, what in its *own Nature* is *best*, and *fittest* to be done; and, being void of all Bias, Prejudice, and Passion, cannot but approve of what is *right* and *best;* and being likewise *Almighty*, no Power can possibly interrupt, or prevent what he determined to accomplish: So that it is *morally impossible*, that God should do an evil Thing, These Truths are so deducible from each other, and in themselves so evident, to all unbiassed and inquisitive Minds, that one would wonder to find Men, of Learning and Integrity, give into the contrary Sentiments; which, in Effect they do, who hold Doctrines *naturally subversive* of these fundamental Truths, as all certainly do, who depart from the moral Good and Fitness of Things, and resolve all into *mere sovereign Pleasure* alone, *independent* of Wisdom and Goodness; which must ever be at hand to *cooperate* with, and govern the Exertion of, their favourite Attribute, *sovereign Power* itself; or, if they do not expressly affirm this, they do by another Method the very same thing; and that is, by denying, in Effect, the *intrinsick Difference* of Good and Evil, which, according to them, has no Foundation in the *Nature* and Relations of Things, but takes its Rise, only, from the mere Will and Appointment of the *Deity*. But if all Things are in themselves equally Good, where is the Use to *appoint*, or the Sense of talking about it? Wisdom and Goodness must, according to this Notion, be idle and unmeaning Sounds, without Sense or Service. But alas! the natural Consequence of maintaining Tenets, so repugnant to common Sense, is seldom less than running into and embracing other Absurdities, in themselves equally great with what they are brought to defend, And here, as some of these Gentlemen are exalted, and I hope deservedly, to the Dignity of Teachers in the *Christian Church*, they will, I hope, permit me to ask them a Question or two, which I should, on almost any other Occasion, blush to ask any rational Man, *viz.* If they do not perceive an intrinsic Beauty and Excellence in Virtue, as opposed to Vice; independent of all *positive* or arbitrary Appointment, tho' of the *Deity* itself; and whether, besides the Commands of God, (which to be sure are of high Importance, and ought ever to be urged with great Strength and Energy) they do not also *press* upon their Hearers, the Practice of Virtue, and endeavour to recommend, and inforce it on the Mind, from its *own* native Charms? But to make this Matter, still, if possible, more evident; let us suppose the present excellent Order of Things inverted, and that God, of his own mere Pleasure, had given Mankind quite contrary Laws, and commanded *Rebellion, Murder, Ingratitude*, and all Manner of Intemperance and Debauchery, instead of their *opposite virtues;* would the same Fitness, Beauty, and Propriety, appear to these Gentlemen, as there now does, in *Virtue?* If not, from whence the Difference arises, let them answer.

As God is an infinite Mind or Spirit, perfectly acquainted, at every Instant of Time, with whatever *hath been, is,* or *shall be;* and all Things *possible to be;* 'tis evident, that all possible Relations of Persons and Things are fully known to him; and that all *moral* and *divine* Obligations, arising from the Relation we stand in to God, and to each other, did, in their own Nature, *previous* to actual Law or Commandment, exist; because the one was in Time, and the other Eternal; one commenced only (at best) with the *Being* and *Beginning* of Creatures, the other was from all Eternity, *co-existent* with the

Divine Wisdom itself; and such an inseparable Concomitant therewith, that, in regard to the *Divine Being*, himself, it was absolutely impossible, but that, on his creating such a Rank of Beings as we are, *moral* and *religious* Obligations must have been *invariably* and *unalterably* the same; and if, as these Men teach, God's having commanded the Practice of Virtue, be its peculiar Sanction, and that *alone* which distinguishes it from Vice or Evil; then, by the same or as good an Argument, his commanding Light in the Beginning, is all the Reason we have for esteeming Light and Darkness different, (as they really are) the one being the actual Pretence of a real Body, and the other a mere Name, to signify its Absence; not that Vice is therefore a mere Name, to signify the Absence of Virtue, for Comparisons seldom hold good in *every* minute Particular; but there is a Parity between the two Cases, sufficient to justify my bringing in the one, as an Illustration of the other. There is no Knowledge *more certain*, than what Mankind commonly have of Good and Evil; and he who, in order to serve any private Scheme of Religion, goes about to depreciate this Knowledge, robs Mankind of all Truth and Certainty whatever, and in the End subjects his own darling Schemes to the same Uncertainty; for if we cannot judge of the Fitness, of plain moral Truth and Duty, neither can we of any Scheme of Religion; especially such as hang together more by Art and human Contrivance, than by Reason or Revelation.

Being very desirous to get all the Information I could, concerning the Matter in Debate; I have attentively read over Mr. *Cole's* Treatise on the *Sovereignty* of God. I know 'tis thought an unanswerable Performance; and, so far as it regards general Christianity, it is worth every Christian's serious Notice: But as to the Doctrine it was wrote to support, it leaves it (in my Judgment) no better than it found it; but is miserably weak, and defective, as to any Thing that looks like sound Reason, or true Argument; and amounts to no more than this *poor Assertion, That because God is a Sovereign, he may do what he pleases:* And, from the Instances he brings from Scripture, 'tis plain, that Mr. *Cole* himself pays as *little* Regard to the intrinsick Worth and Excellence of Things, as is done by many of his Brethren. The manner in which he has been pleased to give us the Story of *Jacob* and *Esau*, proves the Truth of this Observation, I have no great Inclination to spend Time in explaining *hard Passages* of Scripture, (tho' if any thing of that kind can be serviceable, or deem'd excellent, 'tis Mr. *Taylor* of *Norwich* his Book on *Original Sin*,) or to trespass on the Reader's Patience, by throwing one Text of *hard* and *uncertain* Meaning against another; for by this means the Controversy hath been needlessly prolonged. Where the Scriptures are *plain*, *positive* and *reasonable*, their Authority ought to be conscientiously adhered to: But as this is not always the Case, the *next* Thing to knowing what is the *true Meaning* of any particular Text of Scripture is, to know what it neither *does* nor *can* possibly mean; in which Case, the Divine Attributes, and the Nature and Reason, or (if you please) Fitness of Things, is the best Rule. We *cannot*, it is impossible we *should*, understand the certain determinate Meaning of any Text of Scripture *better*, if altogether *so well*, as we do *know* certainly, that God is *just* and *good*, and *know* also as clearly, what *Justice* and *Goodness* mean, when applied to the *Deity*, as we do, when we apply them to *ourselves*. And this Rule, if duly observed, would be abundantly sufficient, to set aside many Interpretations of Scripture, too commonly admitted upon this and the like Occasions. And, besides this never failing Argument (to all who attend duly to its Force) it is worth while, just to remark, that though, as the *Bible* now stands, there are in it (as we must acknowledge) some Passages, which (especially at first sight) seem to favour the Doctrine of *Sovereignty*, &c. yet as it is possible, nay sometimes easy, to give them *another interpretation*, and the general Scope and Tenor of the Scripture being agreeable to such an Interpretation, we have abundantly more Reason to *reject*, than to *admit* of the Sense, in which these Gentlemen are pleased to understand and expound many Texts of the *Bible*, relating to this and other affinitive Points.

I would not, as I observed before, presume to impose on the Reader's Time and Patience, by entering unnecessarily into the scriptural Part of the Argument; yet I must beg Leave, to make now and then an Observation or two as I go along: And the first Thing that falls in my way is, the Story of *Jacob* and *Esau*, and the Account which Mr. *Cole* gives of it. He not only relates the Story, but assures us, that *Jacob's* obtaining the Blessing was of Divine Appointment, and (what is more extraordinary) that the *Falsehood* and *Fraud* he practised to accomplish it, was all of God's own immediate Direction; and this he gives as an Instance of God's*Sovereignty*, and proceeding contrary to the moral Fitness of Things, and the Nature of those Laws he hath given to Man. That God intended *Jacob* the *Blessing*, or preferred him to *Esau*, I readily grant; but cannot admit it to be inferred from thence, that the Means, by which it was, as we reckon, accomplished, were *Divine* also: There is a more natural or (at least) more justifiable way of accounting for the whole Matter. According to the History, it seems plain, that *Rebecca* only, and not her Husband, was privy to this Designation of the *Deity:* she had upon Inquiry (when with Child) received such an Assurance from the Lord; which might be the *first Cause* of her preferring *Jacob* to *Esau*, and which in Time, 'tis probable, grew up into a much greater Degree of *Partiality* and *Fondness:* All this Time the good Old *Patriarch*, her Husband, seems to have been entirely unacquainted with the Affair. And when the Time drew nigh, in which, according (as some think) to Custom, he was about to *bless* his *eldest* Son, *Rebecca* then grew diffident of the Accomplishment of the Promise made in *Jacob's* Behalf, and applied herself to the Means, which the Text tells us was used on that Occasion. As to the Authority those Heads of Families had to *confer Benefits* on their Offspring, by way of *Blessing*, though I shall not now much contend about it, yet give me Leave to make a few Observations. It don't appear to me that *Isaac*, in giving his Blessing, did so properly or so much bestow it on the *Person* of *Jacob* present, as he did on the *Person* of *Esau* absent; because it is the Intention which ought principally to be regarded, and *Esau* undoubtedly was intended. Again, this way of blessing, if considered in itself as a mere Tradition, could be *no more* efficacious, than what now prevails in some Parts of the *Christian Church.* All true Authority of this kind (if any there be) must result from *immediate Inspiration and Command;* and whether *Isaac* had these Qualifications, while *Jacob* stood before him, personating *Esau*, is a Matter of no small Doubt and Dispute. He was ('tis evident) much surprised at the *Cheat*, put on him by his *Wife* and *Son*, and would doubtless very willingly have given *Esau* the Preference, according to his first Intention; but something *supernatural* seems now to have seized and satisfied him, that *Jacob* was the Person intended; for he cries out, "I have blessed him, yea and he shall be blessed." And this latter Assurance, and the Energy and Satisfaction wherewith the Words were pronounced, I take *rather* to have been the *true Blessing* than the *other*. For, as the Reason of *Jacob's* Dissimulation was intirely owing to his Mother's Diffidence and Impatience; so, there is no Doubt to be made, but that the *Almighty* himself would, had she not interfered, have brought it about in a manner becoming his *Holiness*, and not by *Falsehood, Deceit*, and *Dissimulation. Religion* can never be *more* dishonoured, or the Despensations of God to Mankind receive *greater* Reproach, than when *Divine Purposes* are (under God's immediate Direction) said to be accomplish'd by Methods in themselves *evil* and *immoral*, and altogether opposite to His Commands. Hath he forbid us Lying, under the *Penalty* of *Hell-Fire*, and shall he himself practise it, or immediately influence another to do it, for the sake of bringing to pass some Event, which he could as easily have accomplish'd, by Methods purely righteous and honourable! And had *Jacob* never been prompted, or attempted to obtain the Blessing in the manner he did attempt it, 'tis more than probable, that God, who removed *Isaac's* Surprise, and caused him to break forth as he did, "I have blessed him, yea and he shall be blessed," would never have permitted or impowered *Isaac*, to have *blessed Esau*, in an *effectual* manner beyond his Brother: Or if a mere Pronouncing of Words, when uttered as a Blessing from the Heads of Families, was in itself an *irreversible Blessing*, and *Isaac* had attempted to bestow it on *Esau*, God no doubt would have stayed his Mouth by *Intimations within;* as he did, on another Occasion, the *Hand of Abraham*, by an Angel without: Provided, I say, it be allowed, that a *formal Blessing*, from the Mouth of *Isaac*, was necessary to confirm on *Jacob* those superior Privileges, which God had designed for him; and that this Interpretation of the Text is more honourable, and better becoming the Truth and Majesty of the *Divine Being*. I appeal not to Reason only, but to Mr. *Cole* himself: For whatever Influence Prejudice, or Enthusiasm, may have on some Minds, there are certain Seasons, wherein Truth will display itself to the Realm and Understanding of Mankind, and extort, even from the Mouths of those, who sometimes oppose her, the most ample Concessions in her Favour. Take the following as an Instance—*Cole's Sovereignty of God*, Page 41, 2d Edit. "To this also might be added the strict Injunctions that God hath laid upon the subordinate Dispensers of his Law; as namely, to judge the People with just Judgment, not to wrest Judgment, nor respect Persons; yea, he curseth them that pervert Judgment, and will surely reprove them that accept Persons; and shall mortal Man be more just than God? will he, under such Penalties, command Men to do thus, and not do so himself?"

The Argument is undoubtedly equally applicable to the Sin of *Lying*, or indeed to any Sin whatever; and I appeal to every unprejudiced Reader, if any Thing more to the Purpose could be urged, against his own Account of the Affair between *Jacob* and *Esau*, or even against the Doctrine itself, which he writes his Book to support: and this, in Conjunction with my foregoing Arguments, may, I hope, be Answer sufficient for the Use they make of *all other* parallel Places of Scripture.

By this Concession 'tis plain, that Justice and Goodness in God are, by this Author, considered the same as in us; how else were it possible, to understand what the Laws of God truly mean? *Be you perfect, as your Father which is in Heaven is perfect*, is a plain Indication (taking in the Context) of the moral Perfections of the Divine Nature, in Part apparent to us, as the Text observes, from his admirable Bounty in the Creation; *He causeth his Sun to rise on the Evil and on the Good, and sendeth his Rain on the Just and the Unjust*. Though at other Times, when these Gentlemen are hard pinched with the Iniquity and Injustice of their Doctrines, they apply for Refuge to the *Sovereignty* of God, and give strong Intimations, that *Justice* and *Goodness*, when applied to him, are mere unmeaning Sounds, which at best signify, what mere Sovereignty pleases to do, and that when applied to Man, they signify quite another Thing. And this naturally leads me to the second Thing I proposed to consider, *viz.* That allowing the Doctrine of *Election* to be, as they say, resolveable into God's Sovereignty; that God is just such a Sovereign, as this Doctrine supposes, and these Gentlemen take him to be; that they have his Word for their own Election and Salvation; yet even then, there could be no manner of Certainty as to Religion, no Dependance on the Promises and Threatnings of the Gospel; and consequently, the supposed Elect must *beat the Air*, and run at the same or as great Uncertainties, as any other Persons whatever, under the Government of such an arbitrary Being.

I have, to avoid Dispute, proposed this Argument more to the Advantage of the Elect, than I was strictly obliged to do, by allowing them to be absolutely certain, that God has told them, that they are his Elect, and that he will give them eternal Life; which, allowing the Doctrine of *Election* to be true, is generally much more than they can prove, either to themselves, or to others: allowing, I say, the Doctrine of *Election* to be clearly revealed in Scripture, there will be this Difficulty behind, as to the certain Marks of being of that Number. The Scripture must also as clearly reveal the Marks, as it does the Doctrine, or we shall not be able to apply with any Certainty to ourselves. Is believing the Doctrine, &c. and thinking myself one of this happy Number, a Rule sufficient to abide by? If so, no Man who has this Faith, concerning the *Doctrine* and *himself*, can ever depart from it. Yet, there have been many Instances of Persons, zealous in that way, who saw Occasion afterwards to renounce the Doctrine itself, and with it that *imaginary* and *ungrounded Conceit* of their being, for no Reason whatever, God's dear Children and Favourites, and embraced, in its room, the Doctrines of *universal Grace* and *Free-will;* and upon the best Reasons too, for as without the one, God cannot be just, so without the other, Man, being no Agent, can be no Subject of Rewards and Punishments. These very Men were before thought to be elect, by their most spiritual and best judging Brethren, who pronounced them chosen in *Christ,* and unshaken in the Faith; and so indeed they judged concerning themselves: But the Grace of God being once permitted freely to operate in the Mind, it soon expelled that Ignorance, and Narrowness of Spirit, which (even in many well meaning Persons) is the genuine Effect of such narrow Doctrines. If having this Faith be no certain Mark, because a Man may depart from it, what Proof have they? surely none: But allowing them an absolute Certainty, as to themselves, that God hath told them, in Person, that they are his Elect, it will (on their own darling Principle of Sovereignty) amount to just nothing at all; because, as a Sovereign, God may promise one thing, and intend, nay do another, or the contrary; nor can they prove, or have they the least Assurance, he will not thus deal with them, without recurring to other Principles, which will hold equally strong against the Doctrines themselves—To this Dilemma are these Gentlemen inevitably reduced; they must either give up the Doctrines, or part with any Security of Dependance on God himself, as to their own Happiness. It will be *in vain,* here, to refer to the *Goodness of God,* though, on *my* Principles, the Argument would be unanswerable; on *theirs,* it is *stark naught,* and avails nothing. And pray observe the *double*

Dealing this reduces them to; it is something like setting up *two Gods* instead of one, or, which is much the same, ascribing to the *eternal, unchangeable Being*, an inconsistent and contrary Conduct. Here is, *first*, a *mere* arbitrary Being, that decrees, or pretends to decree, by mere *Sovereign Pleasure* only, the Salvation of the *Elect*; but, because such a Being may as well break his Promise as keep it, here is *another* to make *good* the Promise, who invariably acts according to the moral Fitness of Things: Or, if you take it the other way, here is, 1*st*, A Promise made as a mere *Sovereign*, undetermined by, and unregardful of, *all* moral Obligations; and, 2*dly*, The Performance of this Promise is expected, from a Principle of Justice and Goodness; ever conformable *to* the moral Reason and Fitness of Things: And certainly, in either Case, it leaves Things very precarious; nor can the Promises of such a Being as this (I speak it with all possible Reverence to the true God himself) be any thing near so valuable, or fit to be depended on, as the Engagements of a good and worthy Man. And whatever these Gentlemen, to put a more plausible Out-side on their Doctrines, say, concerning the Freedom and Excellence of that State, wherein our first Father *Adam* was created, and the *Possibility* of his having remained perfectly innocent, and the Blessings of eternal Life, which would have been thence derived to all his Posterity, it is plain to me, they generally believe no such thing; but that, on the contrary, God absolutely *willed* and *decreed* the *Fall of Adam*, Mr. *Cole* himself, their great Advocate, is far from supposing the Condition of *Adam* to have been proper for abiding long in Obedience to the Divine Command, or that, had he stood, his Posterity would have thence become *impeccable* and *happy:* on the contrary, he represents *Adam's* Condition as a very weak and imperfect State, by no mean suited to the Temptations, which his Maker knew he would shortly be exposed to, and overcome with; and all his Posterity, *had they been tried one by one, would,* it seems, *have failed as he did,* Page 72. If all this does not amount to something equal to a positive Assertion, that God *willed* the Fall of Adam, and in Consequence of it, the Guilt and Desert of eternal Death, which is said to be thence derived, to *all* his prosperity, I do not know what is, or can be equal to it; and indeed all this, and much more, may easily be resolved into the Doctrine of God's *Sovereignty:* and whoever thinks I have misrepresented their Faith, need only consult their great apostle Mr. *Calvin.* But let me further pursue my Argument, to prove, that tho' a

Man of this *Faith* has God's *own Word* for his Election and Salvation, he cannot, on this Principle of *mere Sovereignty*, reasonably or safely depend on it: My Reason, which is short and plain, I have already given; because God, as a *Sovereign*, may do just what he pleases, *keep* his Promises, or *break* them. There can be no Possibility of evading this Argument, without coming back to the Goodness of God; which is at once to set aside mere *Sovereign* Pleasure, and evidently recurring to the moral Fitness of Things. As much as these Gentlemen are pleased to despise this moral Fitness, and superstitiously exalt the mere Will of God in Opposition thereto; and if the *Goodness* of God proves, that he *cannot* break the Promise he has made to them of eternal Life; it is at least as strong a Proof to me, that such a good Being *could not* possibly make me for eternal Misery, or, which is the very same Thing, will or decree the Fall of *Adam*, and pass the Sentence of eternal Death on all his Posterity; the far greatest Part of whom he leaves, in this Condition, to perish everlastingly, and *miserable* me among the rest!

A Due Survey of the two Cases, or Conditions, of the Elect and Non-elect, may serve to set this Matter in a clear Light, God being in himself antecedent to the Existence of all other Beings, infinitely glorious and happy, could have no Occasion for Creatures to add to his Blessedness; all that we call *evil*, such as Cruelty and Injustice in Man, ever arises from such a *vicious* and *imperfect* State of Mind, as cannot, for that Reason, possibly belong to *Deity*. As the Sources, therefore, whence these Evils arise, cannot be in God; such a Conduct, as these Doctrines suppose, is also equally impossible to proceed from God, whose *only Intent* in creating must be, to communicate Happiness to his Creatures: Creation infers Providence, and to bring a sensible rational Being into this World; and, instead of taking *due Care* of its Safety and Happiness, to *decree* and render it eternally miserable, is in its *own Nature*, much worse than making an absolute Promise of eternal Life to any created being, and *disappointing that Being* of its Happiness, whether by annihilation, or by changing it to another State, or Mode of Being, no more happy than the present mortal Life; 'tis only a Breach of Promise, which, in such a *Sovereign*, is a mere trifle. We have *no natural* Right to Immortality, *much* less to immortal Happiness; it is the mere Effect of Divine Bounty—But, being created in a weak, dependent State, and surrounded with Wants and Infirmities, we *have* a *natural Right* to the Care and Protection of our Maker; and tho' we allow, no *formal Promise* is made on our Behalf, yet the *very act* itself, of creating such Beings, and the Condition we *are* placed in, contains in it the *Substance* of a Promise; and we may be assured, God will have proper Regard to such Beings. If God be gracious enough to *give* eternal Life, to which we have not the *least* natural Right, can he possibly with-hold that which, from our Make and Dependance on him, we have just Reason to expect? and how Much more impossible is it, that he should make us for everlasting Misery! To make *one Man* for Damnation, is much worse, than promising eternal Life to another, and breaking that Promise; he that does the former, cannot be depended on in the latter. Methinks, the very Creation itself, and bountiful Provision therein made, for the Accommodation and Happiness of Man, might assure us, that (Man being made principally for another World) a *proportionate Care* will be taken of his more important and everlasting Concerns. Which presents me with a fair Opportunity, of exposing a Notion these Gentlemen hold, or a Method they have, of interpreting such plain Texts of Scripture, as are brought to prove God's general Care and Providence over his whole Creation; in *particular*, where *David* says, "The tender Mercies of the Lord are over all his Works:" This, if you believe them, relates only to this Life; so I think Mr. *Gill* says. But what then, Is no Inference thence to be made? If God be thus tender, to provide Temporals, how *much more* will he be kind to the Soul, and provide for *that!* 'Tis a natural and strong Way of arguing, and it was our Saviour's own Method of arguing, as the most Plain and Conclusive: "Wherefore if God so cloath the Grass of the Field, &c. How much more shall he cloath you, &c." *Mat.* vi. 30. The Argument rises in one Case, as much above the other, as *immortal Life* is preferable to the present *mortal State;* and suppose any of us should sympathise with a near Friend, under a *small Degree* of Pain and Affliction, would not the same Spirit of Friendship and Humanity have a *stronger Sympathy*, when Affliction becomes more intense and severe? To be tender and pitiful in the least and lowest Matters, and unregardful and cruel in important and everlasting Concerns, is, with regard to the *Divine Being*, a moral Impossibility; 'tis *beneath* human Nature and Prudence, and the Practice of a good Man; And yet these Doctrines teach this horrible impiety concerning the great God himself.

To sum up this Argument: That Being who can make a sensible rational Creature, on *Purpose* for *Damnation*, instead of taking a reasonable Care of it, which, from its Make and Dependance, it has a Right to expect, as much as though a formal Promise were made, may, with altogether as much (*nay more*) Justice, break its Promises of eternal Life, *made* to another Creature of the same Kind; its Claim not being founded in Nature, but built on Promise. As the former would be a more cruel and un-justifiable Proceeding than the latter, he that is capable of doing the one, can have *no moral Perfections* in his Nature sufficient to secure the *Elect* against his doing the other: and on this *wild* and *boundless* Principle of *Sovereignty*, it is possible that, with regard to *Religion*, Things may be quite *reversed* hereafter; the *Elect*, as they are called, made *miserable*, and the *Non-elect, happy*. I think we may challenge the whole World, to shew on this mad Principle the contrary; and why, as well as any thing else, such an Economy may not be resolved into *Sovereign Pleasure*. If God to *Isaac* conveyed such errant Falshoods, by the Instrumentality of *Jacob's Mouth, Why not* make the same *deceitful Use* of the *Bible*, or even of his own immediate Word, in regard to the Elect? If God, as Mr. *Gill* (I think) observes, has two Wills, "One publick Will of Command, and another of Intention, which is private;" Why, with regard to the *Elect*, may he not promise one thing, and intend, nay resolve on another? One would think it impossible, for any understanding Man to judge thus of his Creator, that it is possible he should command one Thing under the *severest Penalties*, and at the *same Time* not only *will* and *intend*, but irresistibly and secretly work to accomplish just the contrary, and (what is amazing beyond Belief) after all punish severely the Creatures concerned, whom he actuates to bring his secret Purposes to pass: If there can be such a thing as arbitrary Power and tyrannical Government, in the very worst Sense of all, here it is. And here certainly is all the *Phrensy, Folly*, and *Tyranny*, which, I told you in the Beginning, the Government of such an arbitrary Being (as these Gentlemen represent the Deity to be) must ever be liable to.

It is evident, that as worthy Sentiments of God and of Religion, better the Mind, and improve the Understanding; so do weak and

superstitious Principles corrupt the intellectual Faculty, and render
the Soul more blind and inhuman, than it is in its natural State,
unassisted and unimproved by Divine Grace. I have the rather
made choice of this Argument, not only because I have never seen it
urged before, but because I think it more nearly affects Men of this
Faith, than any I have hitherto met with. I may be mistaken; but
while it has such weight with me, I cannot but earnestly recommend it to the serious and impartial Consideration of all who profess this Faith, more especially those who preach it publickly to the
World; whose Acknowledgment of what I take to be Truth, or
friendly Animadversions thereon, will be Matter of no small Satisfaction to me: But I must here enjoin one Caution, *viz.* that it will be
a absolutely in vain to produce Texts of Scripture, till this Point is
better settled between us. In the Art of evading Scripture Proofs, I
allow these Gentlemen to be very skilful and expert; nor can I help
believing, that a small Part of the Penetration and Dexterity, usually
exercised on these Occasions, would, in Men of contrary Principles,
or even in themselves, could they be persuaded to think differently,
be abundantly sufficient to overthrow even the Doctrines themselves: They have a peculiar Talent, at misunderstanding; and per-
verting the plainest Text, and rendering those which are difficult
and obscure in their literal Sense, with much Boldness, and without
Hesitation; they stumble in a plain Path at Noon-Day, and walk
carelessly at Midnight amongst Rock, and upon the most dangerous
Precipices. And here I might safely rest the Argument, and make a
final End of it. *Sovereignty*, such an one as they contend for, once
proved, any thing whatever may be allowed to follow, and all Dis-
putations will be utterly in vain. Allow but the *Roman Church* its
Infallibility, and the Truth of other Doctrines will unavoidably follow. Till these Gentlemen, I say, set my main Principles aside, all the
Scripture in the World will be nothing to their Purpose. Not but in
the main the *Bible* is against them; for the Scriptures *reveal* God's
Being and Attributes *more clearly* than they do most Points of Doctrine: the Reason is, because the Doctrines commonly embraced, are
in themselves *not so plain* to Reason, as the Being and Attributes of
God; the latter being generally acknowledged in all Christian
Churches, tho' at the same Time they widely differ about particular
Doctrines, some of which have no doubt been greatly corrupted in
passing through *various Hands* and Translations: and I have been

informed, by much better Judges than I pretend to be, that the *New Testament*, even in these very Doctrines I have been contending against, has, by *some Partiality* or *Neglect*, been made to speak more roundly in their Favour, than the original *Greek*, or best Copies, will support; and that, in some Places, the Meaning of the Original is inverted in the Translation. The Scripture not only revealing to us the *Being* and *Attributes* of God, *more clearly* than it does many Doctrines, and that Fundamental of all true Religion being also in itself perfectly agreeable to the Light of Nature; 'tis evident, we are bound to reject the most positive Text of Scripture militating against this everlasting and fundamental Truth: and rather than part with this, we had much better suppose the Writer, as to disputable Points, to have been mistaken at the first, or the true Meaning corrupted by others. The Translators are allowed to have been fallible Men, and 'tis very probable some Errors might creep in at that Door: But it will not so easily be granted, that the *inspired Writers* could mistake, nor would I suppose it, unless in *very extraordinary Cases*, where either *that* or something *worse* must be supposed; and such a Supposition will, I am sure; much better become us, than to imagine it possible for God to make a Revelation of his Will to Man, which shall upon Examination be found *contrary* to his Being and Goodness, as well as expressly contrary to other *plain Parts* of this Revelation, Tho' the Argument, I say, might be safely rested here, yet as there are some well meaning Persons, who believe that *Adam* was made upright, and furnished with a Stock of Strength and Understanding, sufficient to *preserve* his Innocence; that God made a Covenant with him, as our *Federal* or *Representative Head*, wherein it was stipulated, that if he continued upright, during the Time of Probation allotted, *all* his Posterity should be *for ever* happy; but that if he fell, *all* should be *subject* to everlasting Misery, as the counter Part of the Covenant; and he falling, the Restoration of his fallen Race should be intirely owing to the good Pleasure of God, who might *redeem all* or only *a Part*, and leave the rest to perish in the State wherein he found them, and in which *Adam* had involved them by his Transgression: This they call *Preterition*, or a *Passing by*, which sounds a little better than that harsh Word *Reprobation*, tho' in reality no better at all: And on this first Transgression *some* found the Doctrine of *Election*, and others that of *Infant-Baptism*, as an Expedient to wash away this original Guilt; and it must be owned, the

Virtue of the Remedy is admirably well suited to the Malignity of the Disease. I shall, for their sakes, inspect a little farther into the Affair; to me it appears unreasonable, and therefore improbable, that God should make with *Adam* any such Covenant or Agreement, or suffer the eternal State of all Mankind to hang upon the single Thread of *one Man's* Behaviour, and who too (it seems) God knew would swerve from his Obedience: besides, in all equitable Covenants, *every Party* concerned has a Right to be consulted, nor can they be justly included to their own Detriment, without Consent first obtained, (especially if the Thing covenanted for, has an immediate, or may have a very fatal, tho' very remote, Tendency, to make *wretched* and *unhappy*) which, in this Case, with regard to the Unborn, could not possibly be had. I am sensible the Gentlemen against whom I am arguing (especially Mr. *Gill*) have many pretty Inventions, to justify such a Conduct in the Divine Being, such as producing parallel Instances, drawn from the allowed Practice of Men, and Usage of the State; in particular, the Law relating to *High-Treason*, whereby a *Rebel's* immediate Descendants are *deprived* of inheriting their Father's Estate, with others of a like Kind; to all which, what I am about to offer may, I hope, be a sufficient Answer: The two Cases differ so widely, that it will be no easy Undertaking to make any Thing of this Instance in their Favour; and 'tis very surprising, to find Men of the brightest Intellects, so weak as to argue and infer, from the Laws of *Fallible Men*, to the Laws of an *Infallible* and *Holy Being:* The Inference ought rather to be just the Reverse; for such Institutions as Men, in this weak and imperfect State, may think convenient for their own Sakes, and the Good of Society, to establish and ordain, can be *no Rule* to him, whose Infinite Wisdom and Almighty Power set him *far above* all such Necessity. Nor, again, does this Case come up to the Matter in Dispute: It is true, that the Heir of a convict Rebel *cannot*, according to our Laws, inherit his Father's Estate; but what then, does it deprive him of any thing that was his own before? No; the Law convicts the Rebel, while *in Possession* of his Estate, which it considers as his *own Property*, and which therefore it justly takes away for his *own Offence*. Perhaps, in Cases of Hereditary Possessions, it may seem a little hard, because it prevents the *next* Heir from inheriting; but if there be any Evil or Imperfection in this, we must excuse it, for the Sake of the Intent, which might be for the general Good, the more effectually to deter Men from *treasonable Conspiracies* against their Prince, whereby the Happiness of Society hath been often greatly disturbed, and whole Kingdoms and Countries depopulated: but in this Case, it is not strictly the Heir's, till he comes into Possession; for the Law, by which he may possess hereafter, may be considered as having in it this *particular* Exception, as to the Crime of *High-Treason*, which, whenever it *occurs* as to the *Parent*, renders the Son incapable, &c. With regard to our Laws, we may, in some Sense, be said to make them ourselves, by our Representatives, whom we constitute for that End: and 'tis besides very probable, that some great Men, who formerly possessed Estates, and settled them on the Male Heirs in their Families, from one Generation to another, might help to make this very Law itself concerning Treason, and consequently they could not but acquiesce with this *very Exception* to the Right of Inheritance in their Posterity. But if it be still said to be unjust, though necessary, 'tis no Argument; for it *cannot* be unjust and necessary too: the Law, in this Case, ought rather (with Submission) so far as it unjustly affects a Man's Children, to be alter'd; and if it robs us of the Security, which arises from deterring the Parent, on Account of the Evils which shall afterwards befall his Child, 'tis easy to remedy this, by laying an *additional Punishment* on the Traitor himself; which, as *Self* is much nearest to us all, might better prevent the Sin of Rebellion, If the present Law be just in itself, there can be no Objection to it; if it be unjust, *no Argument* of any Weight can be drawn from it, in regard to the *Divine Being;* who is holy, wise, and true, and so are all his Appointments concerning the Children of Men.

To bring this kind of Reasoning of theirs up to the Point, they should have produced a Law, which subjected the Son (for the Father's Offence) to the *same corporal* Punishment with the Father, and then also they must have proved such a Law to be just and good. But, as these Gentlemen are so fond of bringing Instances from the *Practice of Men* in this frail State, in Justification of their own Doctrine, I shall present them with one or two of my own. *Murder* has sometimes been committed under such Circumstances, that though the Murderer has been arraigned, there hath been no room to condemn him, all Circumstances having concurred, in the Eye of the Law, to acquit him; *will the Almighty therefore acquit him?* Again, on the other hand, in the Case of Murder, things have so fallen out, as to make an innocent Person look like the Murderer, in the Eye of the Law or Court, which has therefore sometimes proceeded to Death itself; *is this Man therefore guilty before God?* I have put these two Cases, purely to shew the Absurdity of such kind of Arguments: and I hope they will consider better of it, and advance them no farther.

If there was such a Covenant between God and Adam, 'tis strange *no Notice* should be taken of it in the Law given to *Adam*, as laid down in the *Bible*, and where, of all Places, we have most Reason to expect it—this must surely have been the fittest Place for its Insertion—Nor is it only absent here, for there is no positive Account of any such Covenant in all the *Old Testament*. Besides, when the Law was given, and threatening (in Case of Disobedience) pronounced on *Adam*, 'twas *merely personal—In the Day* thou *eatest thereof*, thou *shalt surely die*. And when *Adam* and *Eve* had broke the Command, and God descended to judge them for it, their Sentences were *personal* and *particular*, and no reproaching *Adam* on the Account of Evils to be thence brought on his Posterity, and *much less* of eternal Damnation. The *Jews* indeed, many of whom were weak enough to embrace any Absurdity at all, had by some Means contracted a Notion, not altogether unlike this of *original Sin*, probably from a Misunderstanding of the second Commandment, which speaks of "visiting the Iniquity of the Father upon the Children, &c." But 'tis highly worthy of our Notice, that God himself was *greatly displeased* with their having imbibed this Notion, and commanded the Prophet *Ezekiel* to refute it at large; the Substance of which I cannot avoid setting down, it being so full to my Purpose. The Prophet introduces it thus, *Ezek,* xviii. 2. *What mean ye, that use this Proverb in Israel, The Fathers have eaten sour Grapes, and the Children Teeth are set on edge?* Ver. 4. *Behold all Souls are mine, as the Soul of the Father, so also the Soul of the Son is mine: the Soul that sinneth, it shall die.* The Prophet then, from *ver.* 5. to 19. puts the *two Cases* of a *righteous Man's* having a *wicked Son,* and a *wicked Man's* having a *righteous Son,* in order to shew, that neither is the one *better* for his Father's Uprightness, nor the other at all *worse* for his Father's Wickedness; but that all is, as it should be, placed to the Account of their own *Merits* or *Demerits.* Ver. 20. *The Soul that sinneth, it shall die: the Son shall not bear the Iniquity of the Father, neither shall the Father bear the Iniquity of the Son; the Righteousness of the Righteous shall be upon him, and the Wickedness of the Wicked shall be upon him.* Ver. 23. *Have I any Pleasure at all that the Wicked should die? saith the Lord God: and not that he should return from his Ways and live?* Ver. 25. *Yet ye say, the Way of the Lord is unequal. Hear now, O House of Israel, Is not my Way equal? are not your Ways unequal?* Ver. 32. *For I have no Pleasure in the Death of him that dieth, saith the Lord God: wherefore turn your selves and live ye.*

Words more positive against this Doctrine cannot be laid together. *Justice* and *Equity* are here, by the Almighty himself, consider'd as the *very same*, both in God and Man; and the same Justice and Equity, which *He commands* us to make the Rule of *our Actions*, 'tis evident *He here* makes the Rule of his *own*. He blames them for their false Principles, their Ignorance and Bigotry, and is not a little offended, because they thought him capable of acing in so evil and unrighteous a Manner, as that would be, of *punishing the Child for the Parent's Offence;* and strongly and solemnly assures them, he will do no such Thing. And as Justice and Equity would not bear it then, it is plain that, God could never take any such cruel and disreputable Measures, either in the Beginning, or at any time afterwards; because, to act thus at the Creation of Man, and disdain the Imputation with Indignation afterwards, argues a strange Inconsistency in the Conduct of God towards Men; but the Truth is, the same Reasons which made him abhor the Imputation afterwards, could not but infallibly prevent his making any such unrighteous Covenant in the Beginning. What would you think of a Man, who is a Villain to-day, and boasts much of his great Honesty tomorrow? The *Appearance* of *Christ* in the Flesh was, we are told by these Gentlemen, on Account of *Adam's* Transgression, without which it would have been, they say, wholly superfluous. But the Expediency or End of *Christ's* coming, may be resolved into the *Love of* God, on the *one hand;* pitying the Ignorance and Folly of Mankind, on the *other:* and whether this State was the Effect of *Adam's* Sin, or of their *own* personal Demerits, it makes *no Difference* in this Case. Whoever looks carefully into the Evangelists, will find abundant Reason to disapprove and condemn this Doctrine of *Original Sin,* and of *Christ's* coming into the World on *that Account only.* Our Saviour, had this been the Case, would either have plainly express'd, or have given some strong Intimations concerning it: Yet no such thing appears;

but the contrary, to a *Demonstration*, from no less than two Passages of Scripture, recorded by St. *Mark*, (ix. 36.) When the Disciples had been privately contending for Preheminence above each other, our Saviour, to rebuke this aspiring Spirit, sets before them, as a Pattern of Simplicity and Innocence, a little Child; which must have been very absurd, according to the Notion of *Original Sin:* The second is *Mark* x. *ver.* 13. 14. 15. 16. where *Christ* assures his Disciples, that, in order to enter into the Kingdom of Heaven, they *must become as little Children.* And in St. *Matthew* (xviii. *ver.* 3.) this very thing is, if possible, more *Strongly* and *Emphatically* express'd. Which Declarations, had there been such a Thing as the Guilt of Original Sin, *subjecting Children to* God'sWrath *and Displeasure*, would have been ungrounded, and erroneous in a high Degree; for if they were to become like such a little Child, as a necessary and fit Condition for Heaven, the Condition of Infants *must also* be suitable to that Blessed Place—*Suffer little Children to come unto me, and forbid them not, for of such is the Kingdom of Heaven.* The Word Such, is a general Term, equally applicable to all Infants whatever: it shews their Innocence, and how acceptable they are to the Almighty; and, consequently, demonstrates the Doctrine of *Original Sin* to be Spurious and Erroneous: as is also the Practice of *Infant Baptism*, in Support of which, this very Text is wisely alledged; whereas the Text itself assures us, that Children are *already*, by Nature, in that *same State* of Innocence, which *Baptism* is design'd to procure them: and how vain the Ceremony, under such a Circumstance, must be, is *too evident* to need Explaining.

But suppose there was such a Covenant, our Condition, in point of Innocence, is just the same as it would be without it; we could have no manner of Concern with *Adam's* Transgression: and our Innocence in either Case being *exactly* the same, God cannot but look upon us (in our natural State, before we commit Sin) as Creatures that never did any thing to offend him, and consequently be gracious and kind to us; for to leave us in this State, to suffer everlasting Torment, is worse than a Breach of Promise made to the Elect; and if we are as innocent, as tho' no such Covenant had ever been made, God cannot but regard us accordingly: and this proves that such a Covenant could never be made, because to no good or valuable End.

I am fearful of swelling this Pamphlet, beyond its intended Bounds; yet so fast do my Thoughts, on this Subject, multiply and enlarge themselves, that I must beg Leave to Say a small Matter, concerning that *Propensity to Evil*, which we are told is derived from *Adam*, as a Fruit and Proof of his first and original Offence. If *Adam's* Sin had this Influence on his Posterity; as the Act, which produced it, was *one* and the *same*; and all his Posterity standing in the same Relation to him, as their Federal Head; 'tis evident, in this View of the Matter, that *this* Bias to Evil, must in *all* be *uniform* and *alike:* but the contrary seems demonstrable, from undoubted and incontestable Experience; some Children having *much stronger Propensities to Evil*, than others: And if Part of this can be resolved into something besides the *Influence* of *Adam's first Transgression*, and *subsequent* to the *Fall;* it lies (I think) on our Adversaries to shew clearly, why every Propensity to Sin, may not likewise be resolved into something besides, and *subsequent* to, this *original Transgression*. But allowing we are born into the World, with this *Propensity to Evil*, and that we derive it from *Adam's* Sin; yet if God be *merciful*, he could never leave us in this deplorable Condition; nor would his *Impartiality* admit of *redeeming* the one Part of Mankind in a mere arbitrary Manner, and *leaving* the other *to perish*. Nor can much Righteousness be expected from the *Justice* of that Being, whose Mercy can be an idle and unconcerned Spectator, in so very moving, piteous, and Miserable a Circumstance. As to *Adam's* Posterity, where is the Difference to them, whether their present weak and despoiled Condition (as these Men deem it) be the immediate Work of *Creation* itself, or the *Effect* of *Adam's Sin*, and Abuse of his intellectual Powers. We are what we are by *Necessity*, strict *Necessity:* and though it may be called *moral Necessity*, in order to palliate and distinguish it from that which is natural; it operates on us, to all Intents and Purposes, equally the same; and the giving it a milder Name, looks like a sophistical Artifice. If Man's Nature be impaired by the Act of another, God, as a *just* and *good* Being, will either abate of the Rigour of his original Law, or replenish and restore our decayed Powers.

The *same Goodness* (if these Gentlemen will allow it was *Goodness*) which prompted the Almighty to make Man such an excellent and blessed Creature in the Beginning, must also prevail with him, to look even on *Adam* himself with an Eye of Pity and Compassion, after he had sinned; and much more must he be inclined to provide for the *Restoration* of his Off-spring, who themselves had not *actually* sinned, but yet had their Natures impaired by the *Fall*. Besides, if Man was first enslaved by the Devil, not of *Force*, but by *Fraud* and *Temptation*; and Jesus Christ be a kind of *Chieftain*, set up against Antichrist; his Method of *Recovery* must be as extensive as the *Fall* — Why does he save some? but as they are Objects of Mercy, and to recover, with a just Indignation, Souls, originally God's own, out of the Hand of an Usurper, Tyrant, and Destroyer. How can these Reasons operate as to a Part, and have no Influence as to the Remainder? The more I reflect upon the Doctrine, and view it in every light, the more terrifying and deformed it appears: and there is no Argument, short of God's *Sovereignty*, that will relieve the Difficulty; which admitted, will bring on and multiply ten thousand greater Evils.

It may here be proper to take notice of a new Argument, urged in its full Strength, and with all the Advantage of Rhetorick and Eloquence, by the most ingenious Dr. *I — c W — s*, in a Book intituled, *The Ruin and Recovery of Mankind;* &c. We are there told, that this *covenant* seems to have been, evidently, calculated for the best; because *Adam*, in that State of Understanding and Innocence, was more likely to stand, and maintain his Innocence, than any of his Posterity, especially when he consider'd himself as acting for *all* his Posterity; with which the Doctor supposes him to have been fully and strongly apprised; as indeed he ought, had the Case been as the Doctor believes. This Argument I take him to have mistaken both ways, *viz.* by extolling *Adam's* Condition, on the one hand, beyond what in reality it ever was, and setting that of his Posterity much lower than it really is: and these Errors are productive of many others. *Adam* is supposed to have been without any Pain, or Uneasiness, and that he would so have remained, during his Innocence: But after Christ has removed the Curse, and taken away the Sin of his own *Chosen* Children, bodily Pains and outward Afflictions are sometimes their Lot, why might not Man, in his original State of Innocence, be subject, in some Degree, to Pain and Disease? if *Creation* were inconsistent with such a mixt Dispensation of Good and Evil, why not *Redemption?* If God, for the Exercise of Man's Fidelity, placed him where he was exposed to the Evil and Danger of Temptation; why not suffer his Patience to be exercised, at some Seasons, by Pain and Inquietude? To return to this *Covenant,* could it be proved to have been as the Doctor imagines, I see not what could be gained by it: because it would be trifling to a considerable Degree. And all the Arguments, used by *Milton,* in his third Book of *Paradise Lost,* to shew the Absurdity of that Doctrine, which considers *Adam* as *acting,* or rather as *being acted, by Necessity,* in that Situation of Paradise, would be equally applicable to all the Elect, under the absolute Slavery of the *Fall.*

Where is the Use of *Reason,* or *Moral Agency,* in Man, if another be substituted to act in his Stead, and not he himself? Man, being made a *free* and *moral* Agent, has Power to act for himself, and can be accountable for no body's Crimes but his own. The *Consciousness* of being a Sinner, belongs only to him, that *actually* sinneth, or omitteth his Duty. Enthusiasm indeed, which, in its highest Stages, is a kind of spiritual Madness, may have on some Minds a quite different Effect; and the Poor Soul, that is subject to this gloomy and tyrannical Principle, may conceit strange things; it may at one Time imagine itself under the Guilt of *Adam's* Sin, which it never committed; and fancy itself a Saint in Jesus Christ (and what not) at another: it is a mad Principle, fruitful of false Doctrines, Chimeras, and Monsters. It matters not whether (as in the Case of *Natural Madness*) the Reason be lost, or whether (as in that of *Enthusiasm*) it be overpower'd, and brought into subjection to False Principles. The Effect is the same; and between Powers that are suffered to lie dormant, and no Powers at all, there is here no material Distinction to be made. Again, this Notion of *Adam's* being more likely to stand than his Posterity, is a mere Fallacy: it supposes a Difference of State, and Rectitude of Mind, between him and us; which, if true, will likewise suppose, that our State being more weak and defenceless than his, the Task or Duty, assigned us, must be proportionate to our different and inferior Abilities. If *Adam* was put into this State, as *The Ruin and Recovery* seems to suppose, from a Motive of Love in God, to his Creatures, in order to prevent the Misery of the Human Race; the same Love cannot fail to commiserate the Case, and to provide an effectual Remedy for all such as are included in the Covenant. *Adam's* Motive to Obedience must (we are told) have been greatly strengthened by this Consideration, That on *Him* depended the Happiness, not of *himself* only, but of *all his Posterity*. But, I believe, Experience will tell us, that if the Consideration of a Man's own Future State, placed in the strongest Light (as this Book supposes before *Adam*) be not sufficient to move to Obedience, a Regard to others will seldom have any considerable Influence: Such a Covenant enter'd into, or rather arbitrarily imposed on *Adam* by his Maker, could not fail to awaken, in so holy and knowing a Creature, some very uneasy and disquieting Suspicions. This Covenant, and *Partial Election* thence following after the *Fall*, will, if rightly considered, appear very iniquitous and oppressive: because it makes no proper Difference between the *Righteous* and the *Wicked*. If *Adam* had been considered as a private Person only; and *all his Posterity* left to stand or fall, by their own Merits or Demerits; some of those, whom this Doctrine adjudges to everlasting Condemnation, would doubtless have been so *wise* and *happy*, as to have pleased God in their Generation; while others, on the contrary, would have sinned, and transgressed his Laws. The State of the latter is, you see, the same as it would have been, upon the vulgar Notion of *Adam's Sin;* or rather the Guilt of it being, in virtue of this Covenant, imputed to them: The other and better Part, in virtue of this Doctrine, are miserable, and must therefore have abundant and bitter Cause of Complaint against the Doctrine itself. I therefore think it was impossible, such a Covenant should ever be proposed to *Adam;* a Covenant which, if ratified, tended only to make those wretched and miserable, who without it, had they been left to shift for themselves, would have used their Liberty and Rational Powers aright, and have pleased and obtained God's Favour thereby. To talk of its being of general Service, can never be of sufficient Authority to silence this Argument. No *private Injuries* can be excused to *innocent Sufferers* (and much less that of *eternal Torment*) on the Score of general Good; what is it to them, whether *they only,* or *all Mankind* suffer. If *Adam* had stood, these very Men, (who would, had they been left to their Liberty, have proved obedient) would have been in no wise bettered; as he failed, Misery came on those, who would otherwise have been happy. As to those who would, in the Course of their Liberty, have sinned; this Covenant, had *Adam* stood, would ('tis true) have saved them from the Sentence of *Condemnation*. Take it again the other way: *Adam's Fall* could make no Alteration in the

State of those who, without it, would have been Sinners; such as would have proved virtuous and happy, are hereby made miserable. These are, or must have been the Consequences of such a Covenant strictly observed; and the Wisdom and Equity of all Covenants must be judged of, by comparing the good and evil Consequences, necessarily resulting from them. All the Good such a Covenant could possibly pretend to, had it been kept, was, the saving from Wrath such as, without it, would, as free Beings, have sinned; and if, for their Sakes, and to prevent the Evil that might otherwise befall them, such a Covenant was worthy of God to make with Man, a Day of Grace and Salvation, extended for their Recovery, after they might have transgressed, would have been equally worthy of God; and we need not recur to such Fictions and Chimeras. One would think it incumbent on all Legislators, to consider well the Consequences of every Law they enact; for the preferring a Law, whose Consequences can at best be of no Service, and will probably in the main Event of Things be more evil and pernicious than otherwise, would be preferring Evil to Good; in as great Proportion as the Evil might exceed the Good: and how such a Constitution could be better for Mankind, I do not understand. I am sorry any body, especially the Author of *The Ruin and Recovery*, should imbibe and defend such erroneous Opinions, and this too, in Opposition to other and nobler Sentiments of his own, elsewhere delivered.

But, thus it is to be enslaved to the mere Letter of the *Bible*, under a Notion of doing it *just Honour*, when, on the contrary, 'tis the ready way to *dishonour* and *lessen* its Authority.

The Pains which Infants suffer, and the many Miseries to which they are exposed, are, by this Gentleman, consider'd as so many Arguments of the Guilt of *Original Sin*. He thinks that, without such a Supposition, the *Justice* of God cannot be vindicated. [I wish he would stick true to that Argument.] We must, he thinks, suppose one of these two Things: either, *That God punishes them without all Cause or Reason*, or, *That they are under the Curse and Condemnation of* Adam's *Sin:* and the latter is, in his Opinion, the best Sentiment. But I am of a contrary Opinion, and think that in either Case, the *Injustice* is the same. He *allows* it in the *one Case;* and I hope it is *proved* in the other: and really the Picture which this Gentleman has drawn of our young Innocents, is very dreadful and terrifying. If all the *Evils* that befall them in this Life, and *Eternal Damnation* afterwards, be no more than a *just* Punishment for their *Sins*, our *Saviour* must surely have been *greatly out*, in the Encomiums he bestows on their *Innocence*, as I observed before; or, the Kingdom of Heaven, instead of being design'd for *upright holy Souls*, may be a Receptacle for the worst of human Race.

The Brute Creation undergo Pain and Affliction; is *Adam's* Sin, therefore, imputed to them? If not, and they sometimes suffer by Pain and Abuse, why may not Infants do the same? The Miseries of the human Race, reckon'd up and aggravated thro' so many elaborate Pages, cannot all of them be supposed to belong to the *Original Constitution* of Things, but might be partly owing to the Effect of Time and Accident, as well as to the Folly and Wickedness of particular Persons and Nations. This Objection, drawn from the Sufferings of Brute Animals, the Doctor endeavours to answer: I wonder *Adam* is not considered (for the sake of putting an End to the Difficulty) as their Federal Head. He thinks, however, that Brutes must be some way or other included in the *Curse;* and may be punished, as Man's Property: But has Man, because they are his Property, a Right to grieve and afflict them? They were bestowed as a Blessing, for reasonable Service and Delight, not for cruel Treatment and Abuse. The Doctor's Rule of Faith will tell him, *A merciful Man will be merciful to his Beast.* If their being Man's Property will not justify him in abusing or cruelly handling them; it can be no Reason or Argument, why another should do it, even the Almighty himself. Consider Beasts, then, as God's own Property; will that render it a whit more equitable? No: This the Doctor himself, in the Case of Infants, allows would be cruel, and contrary to the Divine Justice and Goodness: and the Argument is the same as to Brutes. But the Doctor, sensible of the Weakness of this Argument, has recourse to another, which I believe will always be admired as a standing Mark of *extraordinary Invention*, to get rid of difficult and perplexing Questions. Brutes may, it seems, contrary to common Experience, have Sensations *less Quick* and *Painful* than ours. I wonder he allows them any Sensation at all; nay, 'tis doubtful if he does allow it. Noise, or Crying out, in them, is, it seems, no Mark of Pain, because some Brutes, under the same Circumstance, remain quiet and still. But will the Doctor say, they have therefore no painful Sensations? Are there no Marks of Pain besides those of crying aloud? Did the Doctor never know a Man sometimes bear a pretty deal of Pain without crying out at all; and give many external Tokens of Pain, at another Time? Did he never perceive a *gaul'd Horse* wince, upon the most gentle Approach of the Hand; and discover Signs of the greatest Fear, and most *exquisite Pains?* Do not some Brutes take as much Pains to avoid the Discipline of the Whip, as tho' their Sensations were the same as ours? I am ashamed to waste Time upon such a Subject; tho' I hope to be pardoned for following so great a Man in his own Method of arguing. He perhaps may continue of the same Mind, and there may be no Hopes of Convincement, till Brutes are taught to speak. By this new Way of Reasoning, the Ground we tread upon, and every Thing around us, hitherto thought Inanimate, may be full of Cogitation. If affording the common Marks of Sensation, be no Proof, that Brutes have it in a common Degree, Wanting the common Marks of Intelligence, can be no Proof that a Stock or a Stone has it not. If I mistake not, Bishop *Berkley* has furnished the World with something equally instructive and philosophical, in relation to the Existence of Matter; which, he endeavours to prove *not* to be a *real*, but an *ideal* and *imaginary Being*. I shall leave others to guess, in what Condition those must be, who think and reason after this extraordinary Manner. But the Doctor has yet another Argument in reserve, to vindicate God's Justice—*Tho' Brutes suffer, yet they may* it seems *have upon the whole more Pleasure than Pain*. But do not some Brutes partake very deeply of the former, in this Life; will the Doctor therefore suppose a Future State for them, by way of Compensation? But this Argument ruins the whole Affair, and may be turned against the Doctor himself, in the Case of Infants, who may be made ample Amends in a future State, for the Evils sustained here, which Evils may have other Causes besides *Original Sin;* for here again, as in the Case of a Propensity to Evil, Pain in Infants, if inflicted because of *Adam's Sin*, must in *all* be *uniform* and *alike*. But the Fact being quite otherwise, some of this Pain and Evil must be resolved into *other Causes;* and if *some*, why not *all?* I grant indeed, that *Adam* himself might have so far corrupted his Nature, as to render him more liable to Pain, than in a State of true Innocence he might have been, and that therefore he might be instrumental to propagate the Seeds of several Diseases, to his Posterity: But had he never done this, his Successors might have done it; and *every Age* has, perhaps, by Intemperance and Lasciviousness, been adding to the common Stock of human Diseases and Calamities: Propensities to Vice might also be propagated in the same Way, and that, and nothing besides, can (I think) account so well for their great and infinite Variety. The Doctor, with the rest of his Brethren, are perpetually urging those common-place Arguments, drawn from the Practice of Men; which in the general I have answer'd already: and, had I proper Leisure, it would be no difficult Matter to give a clear and distinct Answer to every one of them: And these very Gentlemen would, on other Occasions, had they no favourite Point to carry, reject such Reasoning with all the Contempt, and Indignation, it deserves. It is with some Reluctance, I find myself obliged to disapprove the Sentiments of such wise and worthy Grey Hairs, to whom the World hath been long and deeply indebted for his many excellent Services, both from the Pen and the Pulpit. I have read over Mr. *J—s*'s Book, in Answer to Taylor's *Free and Candid Examination;* and tho' I have no personal Knowledge of that ingenious Gentleman, yet I hope he will permit me to say, 'Tis pity, great pity, that fine Talents (pardon the Expression) should be prostituted in the Defence of such an unholy and incongruous System of Religion. Superior Degrees of Learning and Knowledge are, in themselves, most excellent Things, and eminently serviceable, when rightly applied to the Honour and Defence of Truth: But, like a two edged Sword, they cut both ways, and are also too frequently employed in the Propagation of Error.

While I am thus rendering *human Learning*, its just Tribute of Praise, *Truth* requires, that I should be free to detect those little Arts, so often practised to deceive the Unwary, and misguide Mankind. As I am fully persuaded, the Generality of those Writers; who stick by this *Covenant*, and endeavour to vindicate the Honour, Justice, and Goodness of God therein, do it *only* for Decency sake, *and to put* (as I observed) *a more plausible Outside on their Doctrines;* I think it incumbent on me to *detect* this *equivocal* Way of Writing, and shew, that while the Doctor is endeavouring to persuade you he *does not* believe these Doctrines in their most *harsh* and *severe* Sense, there is Reason to suspect he does notwithstanding, *secretly* and *strongly,* believe them in that *very Sense:* nay, he seems to resolve *them* very artfully into the *Sovereignty* and *Majesty of God.* Any Man, who reads the Book, may perceive, how greatly the Doctor is *put to it* for *Arguments,* to answer *Objections;* and he himself knows it to be impossible to make any tolerable or reasonable Defence, of such unreasonable and unaccountable Doctrines: and therefore, lest his *own People* should, from some Expressions, which, at first sight, might look as though he was arguing merely upon a Principle of *moral Fitness,* suspect his Sincerity, he has (Second Edition, *Page* 274) given strong Intimations of his Faith, as follows:

"The Doctrine of *Reprobation,* in the most *severe* and *absolute* Sense of it, stands in such a direct Contradiction to all our Notions of Kindness and Love to others, in which the *blessed God* is set forth as our Example, that our Reason cannot tell how to receive it; yet if it were never so true, and never so plainly revealed in Scripture, it would only be a Doctrine which would require our humble Assent, and silent Submission to it; with awful Reverence of the Majesty and Sovereignty of the great God, &c."

This proves, I think clearly, on what Authority the Doctor himself believes these *Doctrines;* and whoever knows, how *common* it is for Men of *this* Faith, to make a specious Shew of reasoning with others on a Principle of moral Fitness, and among themselves, without Scruple, resolving all into mere *Sovereignty,* will not think I have been too forward or severe in my Observation. I *humbly* presume, what I have offer'd against this Notion of *God's Sovereignty,* is a plain Confutation of the Doctor; and I here, with all due Submission, invite *him,* or any of his *Brethren,* to defend *the Doctrines;* and *this Quotation,* against me. If they *do really* resolve these Doctrines into *God's Sovereignty,* let them speak it out plainly; if they *do not* believe them in this Sense, let them speak that out plainly too; that we may clearly understand, in what *determinate Sense,* they do believe them.

The Doctor has taken a great deal of Pains to make the World believe, that Christ died for all Men, when it does not appear, that he himself believes any such thing. Hear him, *Page* 89, "And methinks, when I take my justest Survey of this lower World, with all the Inhabitants of it, I can look upon it no otherwise, than as a huge and magnificent Structure in Ruins, and turned into a Prison, and a Lazar-house, or Hospital; wherein lie Millions of Criminals, and Rebels against their Creator, under Condemnation to Misery and Death, who are at the same time sick of a mortal Distemper, and disorder'd in their Minds, even to Distraction: Hence proceed those infinite Follies, which are continually practised here; and the righteous Anger of an offended God is visible in ten thousand Instances: yet there are Proclamations of Divine Grace, Health, and Life, sounding amongst them; either with a louder Voice, or in gentler Whispers, though very few of them take any Notice thereof. But of this great Prison, this Infirmary, there is here and there one who is called powerfully, by Divine Grace, and attends to the Office of Reconciliation, and complies with the Proposals of Peace; his Sins are pardoned, he is healed of his worst Distemper; and tho', his Body is appointed to go down to the Dust, for a Season, yet his Soul is taken upwards to a Region of Blessedness; while the Bulk of these miserable and guilty Inhabitants, perish in their own wilful Madness and by the just Executions of Divine Anger."

As I have hitherto troubled the Reader with little Quotation, and it being now so necessary to let us into the *true Spirit* of the Doctor's Belief, notwithstanding any seeming Appearance to the contrary, I hope to be pardoned. You perceive here, that all are called, but the *greatest Part*, in such a weak and imperfect Manner, that is out of *their Power* to embrace the Call, and so they perish as *unavoidably* and *unjustly*, as though no such Call were extended. The Distinction, which is here made between moral and natural Necessity, the Doctor thinks sufficient to silence all Objections, *Page* 285. I have endeavour'd to shew the contrary, and I hope with better Success. Again, what the Doctor observes, *Page* 245, is worthy of Notice, — "Though there must be a *very good Sense*, in which *Christ* may be said to die for all Men, because the Scripture uses this Language; yet it does not follow, that the Doctrine of Universal Redemption is found there: I cannot find that Scripture once asserts that *Christ* redeemed all Men, or *died* to redeem them all."

This is, I think, manifestly a *Contradiction*, and the Doctor, it seems, believes it, only because the Scripture, as he thinks, reveals it. Where is the Difference between *dying to save all Men*, and, *dying to redeem all Men?* And yet *Jesus Christ*, it seems, did the one, but not the other. According to him (the Doctor) the Scripture assures us, that is, the Word of God assures us, both that *Christ did*, and that he *did not*die to redeem all Mankind; which is a flat Contradiction. In what good Sense, I should be glad to know, could *Christ* be said to *die* for *all Men*, when God purposely, and peremptorily, *with-holds* proper Assistances to restore the *greatest Part?* If this be to die for *all Men*, it is certainly not in a good, but in a very bad Sense. But, perhaps, the *Doctor* means, *that Man, consider'd in his primitive Rectitude, has Power sufficient to obey the Gospel as proposed to Sinners, and that* Adam's *Posterity, consider'd as fallen in him, are under the same Obligation to keep the Law, as* Adam *was.* But of this I have already taken due Notice, and therefore I need only put the Doctor in mind of a few Words of his, drop'd *Page* 340, in his *Consideration of the State of dying Infants.* He thinks, "it would be by no Means agreeable, to have them condemned to a wretched Resurrection and eternal Misery, only because they were born of *Adam*, the original Transgressor." This is a rational Sentiment, and I wish it were well improved; for it is better to suppose them entering on a new State of Trial, or downright Annihilation to be their Portion: But what Havock does this Concession make with the Doctor's other Doctrines, of *Christ's dying for all Men in a good Sense, of considering us in point of Obligation to keep the Law inviolable, the same as Adam was before his Fall;* of God's either granting *no Aids* to enable us to *do this*, or such*as are too weak and insufficient to enable us thereto!* We are, he allows, *under a moral Incapacity to keep the Law*, but not a *natural* Incapacity, and therefore God may justly exact our Obedience. But pray consider, if both a *moral* and *natural* Ability be requisite to keep God's Laws, what signifies which of these is wanting, when we may as well be without *both*, as without *either*. It signifies little, what Epithets we bestow on the Word *Necessity*. Wherever it prevails; and whether it be *moral* or *natural*, if it is not *self-caused*, but comes on Man, either by the immediate Decree of Heaven, or by the *Act of another*, it is *Necessity, irresistible Necessity*, and no Distinction can palliate it.

I allow indeed, when Man is created upright, and furnished with sufficient Understanding and Ability to please the Almighty; and yet, *abusing* his Liberty, becomes at length so enslaved to his Passions and Appetites, as to fall into this *moral Debility*, the Law of God is still his Duty to observe: On the other hand, allowing Mankind to have lost their *moral Ability* to practise Virtue in the Fall of *Adam*, and that God, taking Pity upon Man, grants him sufficient

Light, to discern his State, and sufficient *Power*, to obtain Redemption from it, this Man is also under the *same Obligation* to keep the Law of God, as though his moral Powers had never sustained any *Decay* or *Loss* in *Adam;* and I dare affirm, that in *no* other Sense, can Man be accountable for the Pravity of his Will. And let the Doctor observe this, — If it would be unsuitable to the Mercy of God, in the Case of Infants not committing actual Sin, to punish them eternally, *only because they were born of this first Transgressor,* would it not be equally unkind, to leave such as arrive at mature Age, under the Power of those *restless* and *irresistable* Propensities to Evil, derived from *Adam,* and to punish *them* eternally, only because these Propensities, derived in virtue of being born of the first Transgressor, constantly, and *in spite* of any thing we are able, considered in a moral and natural Sense, to do to the contrary, produce *Vice* and *immorality? All* evil Actions, consequent upon this Propensity, are, in fact, as necessary and unavoidable to us, as the Propensity itself, *Where* then, in point of Innocence, can the Difference be, *between* having imputed Guilt and this Propensity, in Time of Infancy, and living long enough in this World, to feel, and shew to others, its arbitrary Effects, in producing Vice and Impiety whether we will or no? and where then is the Reason, for such very different Treatment of Infants and adult Persons? I must observe one Thing — The Doctor and his Brethren, as they make the Work of Salvation, a very easy and agreeable Thing to the Elect, on the one hand; so they assign the poor Sinner a very *hard Task,* on the other: *He that offends in one Point is,* they say, *guilty of breaking the whole Law.* Here is a *plain Instance* of taking *Scripture* in a literal Sense, when it can by no Means be so understood. According to this, a Man, that only *steals,* may be said to commit Murder, and be *punished* as a Murderer as well as a Thief; though we know he has not committed it.

In the main, we may conscientiously observe and keep God's Laws, and yet in Time of *Temptation* and *Weakness* fall into some Evil, will, God therefore *consider* and *punish* us as those who live in the daily Breach and Contempt of all his Laws? No! For, on the contrary, God ever waits to be gracious to all such, as through Inadvertence fall into Sin, and are willing to forsake it. The View and Intent of our Apostle, in these Words, seems to be of very *easy* and *plain* Signification: There was in those early Times, as appears from our Saviour's frequently reproving the Hypocrisy of that Generation, a Sort of People, who appeared zealous in the Externals of Religion, while at the same Time they neglected Things of far *greater Moment:Woe unto you Scribes and Pharisees, ye pay Tithe of Mint and Cummin; and have omitted the weightier Matters of the Law:* Mat. xxiii. *ver.* 23. They daringly violated God's Laws in some of the most material and important Instances, and complied with others in a mere formal ostentatious Way; and were therefore guilty, in the Divine View, of the Breach of the *whole Law;* for *mere Obedience* upon improper Motives to a *Part* of the Law, while at the same Time they allow'd themselves in the *known* and *deliberate* Violation of *more weighty* Commands, was no true or proper Obedience at all: and, in this Sense, the *Jewish* Sacrifices of the Law, though commanded by the highest Authority, were always esteemed an Abomination; and the Christian Religion as well as the Law, is certainly liable to Abuses of the same Kind, from Men of hypocritical and corrupt Minds, whom therefore this Doctrine of the Apostle *effectually* and *peculiarly* regards and reproves: and I appeal to all, if this Construction of the Sacred Text be not more agreeable to Reason and Common Sense, than that which the Doctor has thought fit and convenient to bestow thereon. I beseech the Doctor to consider how, according to his Principles, this Covenant could be proposed to *Adam,* out of a kind and beneficent intention in the Creator, when God knew, in the first Place, that *Adam* would not keep it, and determined, in the second Place, upon the Breach of it, to leave the Bulk of Mankind to perish everlastingly, without Mercy, without sufficient or suitable Means of Redemption; and what a *cruel Joke,* upon the *Calvinistical Scheme,* of God's willing the *Fall,* was here put upon *Adam,* and all his Posterity!

To talk as some do, of our existing in *Adam* at the Time of his Transgression, is very absurd, when, as *intelligent* and *free Creatures,* it is evident, we did not exist at all. *Sin is a Transgression of some Law, which we have at the same time Power to keep.* God never requires Impossibilities. He that made Man, knows best what he is capable of and hath undoubtedly taken care to proportion the *Duties* he requires of Man, to the *Powers* he hath bestowed on him. The contrary would be very hard dealing indeed — If a Law be dispensed to me, I must in the first Place have Understanding sufficient to judge of its

Authority, and the Obligations it lays me under; and, in the second Place, I must also have Power to keep it, otherwise it can never be a Law suitable to me; and a Man's *Age, Complexion, Stature,* and *Circumstances,* are as just Causes for Damnation, as the Breach of a Law which lies beyond the Reach of his Knowledge and Abilities. But supposing, in the last Place, that God did make such a Covenant with *Adam, &c.* (though I think I have shewn it to be impossible) let us see how the Doctrines of *Election* and *Preterition* will turn out *then.* I have already endeavoured to make it appear, that God does not act in that arbitrary Manner, which these Gentlemen teach; that though he is indeed governed by no Law without, or accountable to any for what he is pleased to do, yet his own Rectitude of Mind, is to him an invariable Rule of Righteousness, equally secure to all Intents and Purposes of a written Law without: and this argues the adorable and incomparable Excellency of his Being who, though by Nature he is infinitely above all Power and Authority whatever, yet his moral Perfections continually prompt him to promote the Happiness of the meanest of his Creatures. It was *sovereign Goodness* (rather than *sovereign Pleasure*) which prompted the Almighty to create Man, in order to communicate Happiness to him; and if *Adam's* Posterity might be said to fall in him, yet God must at least look on them in a more favourable Manner, than if they had actually sinned themselves; and consequently it could never suit with his Goodness to punish eternally *any one* under this Circumstance, without *first giving* him an Opportunity of recovering from his lapsed State; nor could he ordain the Means on Purpose to *save some* by *electing Grace,* without *saving all.* God does nothing without sufficient Reason: he could save none under this Circumstance, but as they were *in themselves* Objects of his Pity and Mercy; and if ever there was an Object of Mercy, here it is, an immortal Soul condemned, for the Fault of *another,* which it could by no Means hinder or prevent, to suffer eternal Torment. There is something greatly moving in such an Object as this; and as *all Adam's* Posterity were equally involved in his Guilt, all are Objects of Mercy *precisely the same,* and therefore there is not the least Ground for the Difference which we are told is made by Election; because 'tis making a *Distinction* where there is *no Difference.* Here is the Race of *Adam,* considered as *equally* fallen in him, divided into two very unequal Parts (equally in themselves, and altogether Objects of Mercy, if such an

Object can be) by the Almighty himself. The smaller Number he is at all Events determined to save, and to destroy the greater Number.

In answer to this, I expect to hear that common, but *weak* Argument, drawn from an *earthly Prince*, his extending Pardon to *one* Criminal, and leaving *another* to undergo the Execution of his Sentence. But this is of the same *fallacious Kind,* as that drawn from the Case of *Rebellion,* and shews how *very hard* the Patrons of this Doctrine are put to it for Arguments. Two Men, condemned for one Crime, may not be equally wicked, and consequently *one* may better deserve Pity than the *other,* and to extend it, is in itself a rational and worthy Distinction, made between two *such Criminals.* Let us suppose, in order to illustrate the Argument, that a Man is *compelled,* by Thieves, to go out on the Highway, where he plunders, and is at length, with the rest, brought to Justice; his Sentence would doubtless be the *same* as theirs: But when he is consider'd, as having acted not by Choice, but *by Necessity,* he must needs be an Object of Pity. Nay, mere Justice itself will plead strongly in his Favour. Apply this (so far as it belongs) to the Doctrine of *Original Sin;* which if it makes Men Sinners *at all,* it must be *by Necessity,* there being no *Possibility* for us to prevent it; which is equal to the greatest Constraint that can be produced or imagined, and consequently *all Men* must, under this Consideration, be *at worst* suitable Objects of Mercy. Besides, the Weakness of this Argument will plainly appear, upon considering, with respect to *earthly Princes,* that where the Equity of making a *due Distinction* between one *Criminal* and another, is not the Reason, why *one is pardoned,* and the other *left to suffer;* it *always* arises either from *Caprice, Interest, Solicitation,* or from *Misrepresentation* of Facts to Monarchs; who, too often, *see* and *hear* through *others,* that are not always duly conscientious, to preserve inviolable the Trust reposed in them; and whether such Reasoning as this, can possibly affect the *Almighty,* any Man of common Understanding may easily judge.

But let them apply my Argument on the *Sovereignty of* God against the *Certainty* of their Election, and I believe they will find but little Reason to boast of their Doctrine of electing Grace. They tell us indeed, that this Doctrine of theirs, makes the Death of *Christ* of more Effect than ours, because it secures the Salvation of *some.*

But I have proved there can be no Security in it; and surely that Doctrine, which *puts all* into a Capacity of Salvation, must be better, than that, which leaves *almost every Man* to perish; and if it was better to save a few, than to save none in this arbitrary Manner, it must still have been better and more to the Glory of *Christ*, arbitrarily to have saved all Mankind. They say also, that their Doctrine of Election is a much better Ground for Love and good Works, than is that of *free Grace*. But the contrary is apparent, because whoever thinks rightly, cannot be without this disquieting Thought. — If God, in a mere arbitrary Manner, and without any Regard to previous Fitness, has chosen me, and rejected another; how do I know but his Mind may change hereafter, or that he may not reverse this Decree? or if *unconditional Election* be the true Doctrine of the Gospel, and Man is *equally dear* and acceptable to God *without*, as he is *with*, good Works, what Inducement can such a Person have to please God that Way, when he is already as well pleased without them? If Election is founded upon an *unconditional Decree*, the natural Inference (in all such as believe the Doctrine, and themselves to be of the Elect) must be this — If I am of the Number of the Elect, nothing can frustrate my Happiness; I may gratify my favourite Passions, and wallow in all Kinds of Wickedness, Luxury and Sensuality, and be equally acceptable to the Almighty, as was *David* in the Sins of Murder and Adultery: On the contrary, if I am not of that Number which shall be saved, all my Pains and Obedience will never procure me Acceptance with God, and therefore I *will seek* all possible Gratifications in this Life, seeing it is the only Time and Place wherein I can obtain any Thing like Happiness; nor can the Liberty I take here increase my Misery hereafter, the *precise Degree* of *that* being fixed along with the Decree of my Damnation: Though this Persuasion of being set apart for everlasting Torment, has more often the Effects of Desperation and *Self-Murder*; and indeed the two Extremes of *Presumption* and *Despair*, are the natural Brood and Offspring of these Doctrines, as the reverend and learned Dr. *Trapp* has abundantly evinced, in his excellent Discourse, *against the Folly, Sin, and Danger of being righteous over much*. Hypocrisy and Persecution are also the genuine Offspring of this Faith; and *whenever* it has been tried, Persecution has grown up to a considerable Maturity: for as they pretend to know the Marks of elect and reprobate Men, what can be more natural, than for those, who apprehend themselves to be the *former*, to persecute and take Vengeance on the *latter*. Hath not God, by his own Decree of Damnation, set them an Example? and if he has set a Mark on the Reprobate, they (the Elect) may very reasonably, in Imitation of the *Divine Conduct*, endeavour to make them as wretched as possible here in this Life, and *who shall lay any Thing to the Charge of God's Elect?* I am now shewing, what are the genuine Effects of this Doctrine, not charging Consequences on such as neither do *see* nor *approve* of them: there is great Difference in the Conduct of Men of this Principle; and its natural Effects are, by other Things intervening, often prevented, the chief of which may, I believe, be Want of Power and Opportunity; for tho' many, when out of Power, might be apt to say (as *Hazael* did) *what is thy Servant a Dog, that he should do this Evil?* yet they would perhaps be in some Danger of behaving as that great Man did, when he came to be tried. Some again, who tho' they profess the Doctrine, are yet (I doubt not) often under the Influence of God'sGrace, which, as it tends to humble the Soul, and render it more loving and humane than before, naturally prevents the Spirit of Persecution from taking such deep Root as otherwise it might. And here, though I do not pretend to be a *nice Judge* of the spiritual Part of Religion, yet I have heard such as have been accounted Men of the best Experience say, that when the Grace of God operates on the Soul, the ardent Love of Mankind is *inseparable therewith*. If then the better Sort of those, who profess this Doctrine, are ever sensible of this *most agreeable* and humbling Operation in the Soul, I ask them, if it does not *naturally distend* and enlarge their Wishes, in Behalf of all Mankind? and if this Spirit of Love be the genuine Effect of the Operation of God's Grace, what shall be said of that ineffable and immense Fountain of Grace and Goodness, from whence it proceeds? But, on the other hand, it has been observed, that among mere *enthusiastick and traditional Believers*, of the Doctrine of Election, their Hypocrisy, Deceit and Dissimulation has overtop'd that of all the World besides, even beyond what human Nature could be thought capable of, in its most wicked and corrupt State; in short, they seem to have made the Deceit of *Jacob*, and all other parallel Places of Scripture, that furnish the worst Part of the Lives of good Men, a *standing Rule* of Behaviour — What a blessed Company has the Lord set apart for himself!

The *Foreknowledge* of God is supposed, by some, to belong to the Argument of *Predestination;* but I think it wholly beside my present Purpose, to enter circumstantially into it, for *this Reason* — If, Whatever God *foreknows,* he must also of Necessity *foreordain;* it is manifestly using *Foreknowledge* and *Ordination* to signify just the *same Thing,* and, *in this Light,* every Argument against *Fore-ordination,* must be equally strong against *Foreknowledge,* so far as it affects the Doctrines under Consideration; and when these Gentlemen can shew the contrary, or are willing to enter into the Consideration of the *Divine Foreknowledge,* either *separate from,* or *connected with,* the Doctrine of *Fore-ordination,* I shall always be ready to receive Information.

This Doctrine of electing Grace, they exalt as an *incomprehensible Mystery;* so do the Papists, with as good Reason, that of *Transubstantiation;* for neither of them are Mysteries, or incomprehensible, but *palpable Errors,* whose Absurdity we do *easily and fully comprehend;* nor will the stale Art of playing on the Word *Mystery* amuse us any longer. Another strange Argument, which these Men make use of, in order to set aside some Passages of Scripture, which are positive and express against them, is this, *that if God wills the Salvation of all Men, all must be saved, otherwise we may be said to conquer the Will and Grace of God.* To which the Answer is very easy — Man is made a *free Creature,* and therefore God deals with him as such; because to make him free, and then arbitrarily *overrule* his Freedom, would be making him free to *no Purpose.* The Will of God is sometimes *positive,* and sometimes *conditional.* He gives Laws, commands us to keep them, and promises eternal Life to those who obey; nor can we suppose he commands us to obey, without willing our Obedience. We may indeed *resist* the Operations of his Grace: but to talk of *conquering* God, is Nonsense. He has made us free Creatures; he wills our Salvation, and has granted us such Aids as are sufficient, if we use them aright, to bring us to Happiness: This Conduct in the Divine Being, is not only reasonable in itself, but *perfectly agreeable* to many *plain* and *express* Parts of Scripture. The *Weeping* and *Lamentation of Christ* over *Jerusalem,* is a strong Proof of it: *How often would I have gathered thee, as a Hen gathereth her Chickens under her Wings; but thou wouldest not!* Here was all done, that was fit and convenient to reclaim free Beings; not only proper Aids offer'd, but offer'd in the *most tender* and affectionate Manner, as is evident from the Comparison of the Hen, &c. and by the Words *how often*, is set forth the *great Patience and longsuffering of God:* And notwithstanding all this, they resisted to their own Destruction. God *willed*, or would have saved her, but she was stubborn and rebellious, and would not accept of Salvation; did she therefore *conquer* the Almighty? Suppose my Father gives me a good Education, a good Employment, and a competent Portion in Money, and, besides all, is continually at hand, ready further to advise and assist me, whenever it may be necessary; yet I am obstinate and disobedient, and, by pursuing evil Courses, fall into Poverty, Contempt, and Ruin: I may indeed be said to *resist*, but in no *good Sense* to *conquer* my Father. Besides, according to this absurd Way of arguing, if God does all in Believers, his Laws are to be *kept* by himself; with what Propriety then can they be said to be given to Man? He to whom the Law is given is to keep it, not the Being who gives it.

I might here, very naturally, speak concerning the Sacrifice of *Christ's Death*, and *his Righteousness* imputed to us; but I shall not now discuss it fully, only a few Remarks may not be impertinent or useless. These two Points appear to me to be much misunderstood; *Sin* is said to be infinite, because committed against an infinite God; and that therefore nothing but an infinite Being can satisfy the Justice of God for it: A fine Story indeed, for Men to amuse us with, who pretend to believe in *only one* God: Here is *one* infinite Being, to be satisfied for Sin; and *another*, to satisfy him. And, what is still as bad or worse, it supposes, that an infinite Being may, for a certain Season, suffer or undergo a Diminution of its Happiness; which, in an infinite and unchangeable Being, I take to be impossible. Was it then *only* the Person, or *rational Soul* of *Jesus Christ*, that suffered, being upheld under it, by the infinite Being himself? If so, what is become of the infinite Being, that was to *suffer* for Sin; for does God make Satisfaction to himself? 'Till these Gentlemen either renounce, or better explain this Matter, they will, I hope, think very favourably of all who deal in absurd Schemes of Faith.

The Thing productive of these Absurdities, is a *wrong Notion* of Sin, and of the Justice of God: Sin, they say, is infinite, because *committed against an infinite God*. It is doubtless sometimes a great Aggravation of it, that it is committed against God; but it is not so much his *Greatness*, as our abusing his *Goodness*, that aggravates the Crime: As may appear from this short Observation, That any Favour, disinterestedly done, by a Person of the meanest Rank in Life, lays the Receiver under the same Obligation, as though it were granted by the greatest Man upon Earth: It is the Motive and the Action, put together, that gives it its proper Value to the Receiver. God's Authority may add some kind of Sanction but no Alteration of outward Circumstances, in him who confers a Benefit, can ever after change the Nature of the Action, or the Obligations resulting from it.

And, when we consider, on the other hand, that Sin is committed by a frail finite Being, very often in its unguarded Moments, prompted by Passion and Appetite, and surrounded with the most powerful Temptations; this proves more strongly, that it cannot be infinite. By the *Justice* of God, is not meant, that he cannot forgive Sin without Satisfaction, but that he *will* not punish the Innocent; He proposes himself as a Pattern for our Imitation, and bids us *forgive our offending Brethren, if they repent and desire Forgiveness:* and he himself will therefore forgive on the same Terms; for unless Sin becomes so enormous, as to make Punishment necessary, *Repentance* and *Amendment* is all that God expects. The Gospel is proposed to Sinners, on these Terms; and as to the Death of Christ, it were unreasonable to think, he laid down his Life by way of Satisfaction to Offended Justice, in the Manner these Gentlemen understand it; but in Testimony of the Truth of his Doctrines, and Confirmation of God's *great Love* to the World. This was the Cause of Christ's Coming in the Flesh. God so loved the World, that he sent Christ to save it, by such Preaching and Miracles, and other internal Aids, &c. as were in themselves sufficient to beget Faith in such as gave a proper Attention; such a Faith, in the Soul, as was productive of Morality and Virtue in Practice. It was an *original Act* of Grace and Goodness in God, to send Christ into the World, to save Sinners, and not (as some superstitiously teach) a mere Compliance in God the Father (and that, not without full Satisfaction first made) to the *voluntary* and *merciful* Intercession of Christ the Son. For then our Salvation would be *owing only* to the Love of Christ, and not *at all* to God's Love, who is here considered as a *rigorous* and *unrelenting Creditor*, that will not release the Debtor, until full Satisfaction be made; so that Christ becomes our Creditor, and God has no farther Demand: and what Need then can there be of Intercession to God on our Behalf, when the Debt is already paid, and full Satisfaction made? Christ's coming into the World was *entirely owing* to the Father's Mercy. His Doctrine, Miracles, &c. were what he had in Commission from God, as a Means to instruct and make the World happy; it is he who, instead of being averse to forgive frail Man his Offences, has through Jesus*proclaimed Pardon* to *all*, on Condition of Repentance and Amendment; and thro' the Love of God it was also, that Christ was appointed a Mediator for sinful Man: So that the whole Affair arose from God's own Mercy.

I stand amazed at the Gentlemen, against whom I am arguing; what a *Scope* do they give to the *Sovereignty* of God, in the Doctrines of *Election* and *Reprobation?* And yet they won't *suffer it* at all to operate, in the Case of *forgiving Sin*, on the Terms of Repentance and Amendment. A small, yea *very small* and reasonable Allowance, in regard to the *Exertion* of this Attribute, and in a *good Cause* too, would be sufficient to justify the Mercy of God, in forgiving Sin. If, as a Sovereign, he punishes where no Sin is, surely he may also, as a Sovereign, forgive Sin. So that this Notion of the Impossibility of God's forgiving Sin, without Satisfaction first made, is erroneous and despicable. Repentance and Amendment in the Creature is, in the Nature of Things, a *much better* Satisfaction, than can be made by the Act of another. By the *Justice* of God, I repeat it again, is meant, that he will not punish the innocent, and not that he cannot shew Mercy to an offending, repenting, penitent Creature, unless another sheds his Blood for an Atonement. Nor is the Righteousness of Christ, *strictly speaking*, imputable to any one. The Terms of the Gospel are, *Repent, and be converted, and your Sins shall be blotted out:* Be *sorry* and *amend*, and I will *forgive* you. *The Prayer of a Righteous Man availeth much;* and God, in some Cases, to shew his Regard to the Righteous, and to excite others to become righteous also, may possibly grant *that*, at the Request of such a righteous Person, which without, it might be improper to grant; and Christ being our holy and righteous Mediator, God may do more at his Request, on our Behalf, than he would do without it. Not but that (*independent of* and previous to the Intercession of Christ, at least to the Account we have of it, in the New Testament) God was *ever disposed* to be favourable to Man, and always ready to receive him, coming to him in a proper and becoming Manner: For even this very Christ, and his Intercession, &c. is all ultimately the Act of God, and flows from his unbounded Love and Goodness to Man. So that *imputed Righteousness* can mean no more, than God's forgiving us, at the Request of Jesus Christ (whom he sent on purpose to make that Request, and to do every thing for the Benefit and Happiness of Man) and not a *real Transfer* of Christ's *personal* Righteousness, which is not only in itself impossible, but would, if true, take away all Necessity of our becoming holy. The Righteousness of Christ is altogether different to what these Men take it to be; it is a real State of Righteousness, wrought in the Soul by the Operation of Christ's *Spirit*, Man submitting thereto. I know there are some Expressions in the *New Testament*, which (if precipitantly understood, without Regard had to the Nature of the Thing, and to other plain Texts) seem *a little* to favour these Doctrines. I can't say, by what Means *precisely* the *Bible* came into its present Condition; many Things might concur to give us wrong Apprehensions of its true Sense and Meaning, He that understands human Nature will find, that Men, who have been *great Bigots* in any Way of Religion, *will generally retain* some of their former Prejudices, even after, in the main, they may have changed their Principles, Prejudice in Education is a Leaven, not so easily purged out, as some may imagine; and 'tis possible, the *Writings* of St. *Paul* may have in them a Tincture of this kind; besides what may have since crept in, by Partiality or Accident: against which, and *all Errors* of a like Kind, a due Regard to the *fundamental Principles*, I have endeavoured to inculcate, will, I hope, abundantly secure us. These are some succinct Observations, that I could not well avoid making; which perhaps may shortly be followed by something more *full* and *comprehensive*, concerning the *Virtue* and *Extent* of Christ's *Death*, and the Nature of *imputed Righteousness*. What I have here delivered, concerning God's *Sovereignty*, is not the Result of a few, hasty, or loose Thoughts, but the Effect of long and mature Deliberation. I have weighed over and over the Arguments in my own Breast, and tried their Strength with People, the most likely to afford me Satisfaction; and could I have found it in either Way, the World had never been troubled with these *Free and Impartial Thoughts*.

Permit me, before I make an End, just to observe, in Regard to the Controversy, between Mr. *J—s* and Mr. *Taylor*, on the Scripture Doctrine of *Original Sin;* that Mr. *J—s*, as well as Dr. *W—s*, lays great Stress on that frivolous Distinction, mentioned a few Pages back, of *moral* and *natural* Necessity, to that Degree, that Mr. *Taylor* is treated somewhat *rudely*, for not perceiving the Force of it; when I dare aver, *none* but misguided Zealots, could ever see any Reason or Argument in it: Nor do some of these very Men, who urge it, seem to believe it themselves. Ask them how Man can be justly accountable for Evils, that proceed from a *Nature depraved in* Adam, and they immediately leave *this Distinction*, and recur to the *Covenant;* and this Covenant they cannot support by any Argument short of God's*Sovereignty*, which they are welcome (if they can tell how) to improve to their own Advantage.

To say that Man, in the Fall, has natural Powers to act rightly, and is therefore condemnable when he does not, tho', by Necessity; he wants Inclinations to be virtuous, would, to *use* Mr. *J—s's* genteel Language, *be a senseless Falshood, and shew Poverty of Argument* (I am loth to add as he does) *and Effrontery too.* Such Rudeness deserves Lamentation as well as Reproof, nor do I on this Occasion set before *him* his *own Words* with any secret Pleasure, but purely to shew Mr. *J—s*, how agreeable such a Liberty will appear, when, in return, it may be offered to himself.

Why is this favourite Distinction urged, unless it be to shew, that because Man has natural Powers, 'tis his *own* Fault, if he does not employ them aright; but how does it appear, that such a Power *only*, can render *Man* a whit better, or *more* a *moral Agent*, than he is, or would be, without it? If Inclination to *Virtue*, must *precede* every truly virtuous Action; and Man's Depravity under the Fall, be *such* as prevents his ever having such good Inclinations, his natural Ability to do Good, must needs be a mere *Joke* and a *Cypher*. Just the same as, on the other hand, would be, the strongest Inclinations to Virtue, and *no* natural Power of complying with them in Practice. As nothing short of *Knowledge* and *Power,* Power of both kinds, *natural* and *moral*, can constitute Man a *moral Agent*, or proper Subject of *Law*, of Rewards and Punishments, either here, or hereafter; one would wonder to see this insignificant Distinction urged at all in this Controversy: for it is, at the best, a mere *Parade of Words;* which prove nothing, except it be the Want of Truth and Righteousness, in this Doctrine of *Original Sin;* or great *Bigotry*, and Defect of Understanding, in its most accomplished Patrons. And after all that is, or can be said, concerning *natural* and *moral* Powers; it is doubtful, if such a depraved miserable Wretch, as Man under the Fall is said by the *Assemblies Catechism* to be, can (strictly speaking) have any Power at all over his own Thoughts and Actions; The immediate Cause and Spring of Action *is* the *Soul,* to which the *Body* is subservient only as an *Instrument,* but has in itself, according to the best Philosophy, no Power to produce *voluntary* or *self Motion.* What is called *natural* Power in Man, as opposed to *moral*, is at least, a Power lodged in the Soul, to give Motion to the Body. But these *Volitions* of the Mind, and the immediate Act of the Soul upon the Body, in order to produce *Virtue*, depending on the Mind's being in a State of *Freedom*, able to chuse and prefer Virtue, as better than Vice; it is evident, that in a Mind, totally abandoned to Evil, *moral* Motives have not their due Power over the Man; and what we call his *natural* Power to be virtuous, is either suspended, or quite overpowered, by an evil and irresistable Turn of Inclination, arising from the *Act* of another; I mean, *Adam.* Man then, considered as a *moral* Agent, has Power to *do*, or *not* to *do*, the very same Thing; be it good or evil. But this Liberty of Choice and Action in the Creature, as the *Soul* is but one, and also *the* immediate Source of all Action in Man, cannot properly, I think, be called *two* distinct Powers, but rather *different Applications* of *one* and the *same Power* lodged in the Soul. On the other hand, in such a *depraved Creature*, as Man under the Fall is said to be, the Power of *choosing* and *refusing*, of being virtuous or vicious, which he *pleases*, is altogether lost and destroyed; and such a Man, so far from having *natural* and *moral* Powers, has (properly speaking) *no Power* at all remaining: all his Thoughts and Actions, like those of a Machine, are merely involuntary; he is constantly impelled by something mightier than himself, and ever necessitated to think and act as he does: his being an intelligent Creature, doth not alter the State of the Case, or render him more an Agent than a Stock or a Stone. In this sad Condition, Man can have no Power at all to love and pursue Virtue, untill the overruling Principle, which determines all his Thoughts and Actions to the contrary, be removed, or he receive Superaddition of Understanding and Strength agreeable thereto. My natural Strength of Body may be equal to four hundred Weight; but what can this avail, while I am continually pressed down by four thousand? and all Mr. *J—s's* Skill and Criticism (*Pages* 71, 72) will not evade this Reasoning. The Distinction between immediate and remote Causes of Sin, is as trifling and inconclusive, as the 'forementioned Distinction of *moral* and *natural* Powers. Those indeed, who can fancy themselves to be God's own dear and elect Children, may reject all Opposition with *Scorn*, and without *Examination*, and acquiesce readily in the most rigid and tyrannical System of Religion, that renders the Bulk of Mankind miserable, while the Elect may think themselves secure in the Divine Decree, *with an humble Assent, and awful* (it should be superstitious) *Reverence of the Majesty and Sovereignty of the great God.* But what Reason or Recompence will that be to *him*, who under proper Means and Motives would have kept the Commandments, and so have entered into Life; who would have loved the Lord his God, with all his Heart, Soul, and Strength; and his Neighbour as himself? Or how can such a partial and tyrannical Doctrine, be reconciled to the Voice of Reason in Man, to our common Notions of *Right* and *Wrong*, to the General Scope and Tenour of the *Holy Scriptures*, or to that Text in particular, which assures us, that *the Almighty doth not grieve nor afflict the Children of Men willingly?*

FINIS.